CHRISTIAN
BEING
AND
DOING

Clifford Walter Edwards

Christian
Being and Doing

A Study-Commentary on

JAMES
and
I PETER

PREPARED BY
JOINT COMMISSION ON EDUCATION AND CULTIVATION
BOARD OF MISSIONS, THE METHODIST CHURCH
475 RIVERSIDE DRIVE, NEW YORK, N. Y. 10027

And the King will answer . . . "Truly, I say
to you, as you did it to one of the least
of these my brethren, you did it to me."

MATTHEW 25:40

Recommended Materials

for the study of

JAMES *and* I PETER

TEXT: CHRISTIAN BEING AND DOING: Study-Commentary on James and I Peter. Clifford W. Edwards. $1.00

GUIDE to *Christian Being and Doing*. Ethlene Sampley.
50 cents.

JAMES THROUGH JUDE (RSV pocket edition) 3x4½ inches.
5 cents.

PRAYER CARD: I Am no Longer Mine Own but Thine.
5 cents.

MORALITY, U.S.A. Reprint from *Look* magazine. 15 cents. Order from *Look*, 488 Madison Avenue, New York, N.Y., 10022.

Additional Materials

GOD'S WORK IN OUR TIME. Playlet. Coy B. Howe. 1 act, 14 characters.   30 cents each; 4 for $1.00.

GOD'S PLAN FOR YOU. Leaflet.   3 cents; 10 for 25 cents.

THE LIVING ART OF WORSHIP.   Clarice Bowman. 75 cents.

TO SERVE RIGHT GLORIOUSLY.   Free for postage.

PRAYER CALENDAR.   60 cents.

FLORENCE ALLSHORN. J. H. Oldham. $1.75.

WORSHIP RESOURCES.   20 cents.

TWO OR THREE TOGETHER. Harold W. Freer and Francis B. Hall. $2.50.

A TESTAMENT OF DEVOTION. Thomas R. Kelly. $2.00.

Contents

viii

Foreword

IT IS HOPED THAT THIS STUDY-COMMENTARY ON JAMES AND I Peter will confront the reader with the life-and-death urgency of the Bible's call to mature discipleship in desperate times. By focusing upon the words of two of the often neglected New Testament books, both written for times of crisis in church life, this commentary seeks to arouse contemporary Christians to new depths of Christian conviction, new seriousness in Christian action.

The Book of James was written in a time of moral decline, when professions of faith were failing to find fulfillment in deeds of love. James speaks directly to the false assumption that one can have faith without works, or be worthy of the name of "Christian" without a life of obedience.

Has there ever been greater need for such a message than there is today? Once called an "epistle of straw," James may well be for us an "epistle of rock" especially designed to shatter our day's comfortable illusion that discipleship makes no sacrificial claims upon us in the larger issues or the little honesties of life.

James speaks of such contemporary problems as snobbery, malicious gossiping, money-madness, and weak resignation to society's ills. He attempts to deal with such basic problems as the meaning of human suffering, the origin of evil, and the nature of Christian discipleship. His words lead us to confront with new seriousness the agonies of incessant warfare, separated races, starving peoples, poverty and affluence, crowded mental hospitals, and the man-made world of illusory comforts and securities which ignores God-given human dignity and person-to-person concern.

The simple and pointed demands which James utters are so clear and incisive that they are bound to "bother" us and cause us to lose sleep when we consider our easy compromises with "the way things are done" in this world. The beginning of our cure may well be a goading pain that will not let us rest as long as there remains the terrible gulf between our *claim* to believe and our *will* to do; between the title "Christian" and obedience.

I Peter, which follows James in that grouping of New Testament books called the Catholic Epistles, provides the perfect background for James' urgent call to complete discipleship. I Peter takes us back to the very foundation of Christian faith. It examines the meaning of our baptism and our life within the community of faith, reminding us that Christian *doing* can only take place where there is Christian *being*.

I Peter is like a richly woven tapestry dominated by two major motifs: (1) God's act (the gospel) and (2) Man's response (the Christian life). God's act, the reconciliation of man to himself through Christ's sacrificial death, is the cause and motive power for man's response —our joyful obedience to God's will, the Christian ethic. It is at the point *where God's act and man's response meet* that *Christian being* comes to birth and a life of *Christian doing* results.

Interwoven with these major motifs are other Christian affirmations. Baptism, the sacrament which marks the birth of *Christian being,* has a vital place in this tapestry. Adding to the pattern of I Peter's message are its call to the church to share in Christ's sufferings, its Christian code of social ethics, the paralleling of the history of the New Covenant to the Old, and a description of salvation so all-embracing that it reaches even "the spirits in prison." Woven throughout is a series of descriptions of the Christian community: the church is portrayed as dispersed exiles, as newborn children, as a house of living stones, a chosen race, a royal priesthood, and the flock guarded by the chief Shepherd.

Finally, one must not overlook that affirmation which perhaps best expresses the uniting of God's act to man's response in the disciple's life. Man's response follows the pattern of God's act in Christ: ". . . Christ also suffered for you, leaving you an example, that you should follow in his steps" (I Peter 2:21 ff.). The life of discipleship is patterned after God's own sacrificial involvement in our world through Jesus.

Christians, Peter contends, are citizens of a new land, aliens and pilgrims in this present world. The Christian's responsibility in this world is therefore all the more awesome, for his life must demonstrate to this present world that there is the possibility of "a higher loyalty which will not conform to the popular sins and self-satisfactions of earth." Further, the Christian has a special freedom to become involved in a transforming way on behalf of this world, for he alone is already "owned" by Christ, and so cannot be purchased by the selfish interests of the world.

The Christian, born into a new and living hope, need not fear the disappointments and boredom which beset a world attracted by limited and ephemeral hopes. His hope focuses not upon personal comforts, accumulated belongings, and temporary securities, but upon the consummation of God's plan for his universe. He recognizes, however, that in the fulfillment of God's unfolding plan in history, a very special responsibility has been assigned to him as a member of the witnessing household of faith. Thus he is encouraged to become deeply involved in the world's needs, and is prepared to meet opposition and suffering with "exalted joy." His trust in God's new order allows him to rejoice even during present trials, for "faith is the Christian's key which opens the door to the future and allows the light of the larger room to illumine a new dimension of present existence."

Both James and I Peter were written to church congregations in desperate situations, urging them to grow up in their discipleship. We are now living in an age called post-Christian by many, an age in which the church's very existence is being called into question. Could it be that James' and I Peter's calls to full discipleship, to a rediscovery of the meaning of Christian *being* and *doing*, have suddenly become the most relevant words in the world for us? Through a direct confrontation with James and I Peter, it is hoped that there will be those who *will* respond to their challenge and bring about a new age of Christian being and doing.

APPRECIATION. Special thanks are due to many who have contributed to the preparation of this book.

A long line of pastors, beginning with the Reverend Harold Jones, saw to my early training in church life and Bible study. The people of my hometown church in Southampton, New York, and the parishes I have served in Alto and Bowne Center, Michigan, and Marshall, Wisconsin, continued that training. Dr. Ernest Saunders of Garrett Theological Seminary and other professors too numerous to mention here have patiently instructed me in many of the necessary disciplines involved in understanding the Bible and its relevance for the Christian life.

Thanks are due to Wesleyan College, Macon, Georgia, for providing aid and the environment in which most of this book was written. The library of Central Baptist Theological Seminary in Kansas City, Kansas, also helped much by graciously allowing me to use its facilities for research during an entire summer. My wife has also played an essential part in this work through her suggestions, typing, and proofreading.

Clifford W. Edwards

Wesleyan College
Macon, Georgia
December 19, 1965

THE BOOKS OF THE NEW COVENANT
[THE NEW TESTAMENT]

The Gospel according to

>MATTHEW
>MARK
>LUKE
>JOHN

The Acts of the Apostles [or Part II of Luke]

The Letters of Paul to the

>ROMANS
>CORINTHIANS, I AND II
>GALATIANS
>EPHESIANS
>PHILIPPIANS
>COLOSSIANS
>THESSALONIANS, I AND II
>TIMOTHY, I AND II ⎫ CALLED THE
>TITUS ⎭ PASTORAL LETTERS
>PHILEMON

Letter to the HEBREWS

Catholic Epistles [or General Letters] of

>JAMES
>PETER, I AND II
>JOHN, I, II, AND III
>JUDE

The REVELATION to John [or Apocalypse]

1

Introducing our Study

"I'VE ALWAYS MEANT TO GO AND LOOK MYSELF"

Robert Frost's poem "The Mountain" tells of a visitor who is intrigued by a mountain which dominates the landscape for miles around. Stopping a local villager who has farmed all his life at the foot of that mountain, the stranger asks him how best to climb it and what one will find at the top. The local villager, however, knows little more about the mountain than a few rumors he has heard, and confesses:

> . . . I've always meant to go
> And look myself, but you know how it is:
> It doesn't seem so much to climb a mountain
> You've worked around the foot of all your life.[1]

I

As Americans we do "know how it is." We often take for granted or ignore wonders close at hand although we will go out of our way to visit lesser places made attractive by their distance.

The landscape of our history and culture has been dominated by the Bible. The Bible has always been close at hand, echoed in our nation's earliest documents, in spirituals and folk songs; read at baptisms, marriages, and funerals; placed on our living-room tables, in our churches, hotel rooms, and store windows. Most of us have worked around the foot of the Bible all our lives, glimpsing a verse here or taking a few lessons there. Yet a questioning visitor would probably find that, like Robert Frost's farmer, few of us could guide him to the Bible's heights and describe its trails and wonders; for, though we have tiny bits of information and second-hand rumors, few of us have done the hard work of climbing the Bible's peaks and learning its trails for ourselves. It just hasn't seemed so much to climb a mountain we've "worked around the foot of" all our life.

Visitors to Christianity, new converts, and far-off tribes often shame us by their excitement on discovering the Bible for the first time. It is sometimes hard for us to understand why a tribe will clamor for the Bible to be translated into its own language, or what pressing need could lead a man like Tyndale to give his life to make the Bible available in English, or why Englishmen of the sixteenth century lined up in

[1] Robert Frost, "The Mountain," *Complete Poems of Robert Frost*. (Copyright 1930, 1939 by Holt, Rinehart and Winston, Inc. Copyright 1958 by Robert Frost. Reprinted by permission of Holt, Rinehart and Winston, Inc.)

the parish church in order to take their turn at reading from the Great Bible chained to the lectern. The great Indian leader Gandhi, who was not a Christian but a Hindu, is said to have been so impressed by the words of the four Gospels that he committed them to memory! How many among us, who claim the Bible as "our Book," have ever been so moved to appropriate what it has to say?

Probably it is not indifference so much as a too casual familiarity which has led most of us to take the Bible for granted and hence never to study it seriously for ourselves. How many of us could echo the words of Frost's poem: "I've always meant to go and look myself . . . "?

This study is meant for those who have intended to look into the Bible and its meaning for life and are now setting out to do so.

It is hoped that we can put away our casual familiarity and explore at least a part of that mountain, the Books of James and I Peter, with a sense of excitement and discovery. Those more experienced in this venture should be of special help, for, not unlike mountain climbers, we are all bound together and we must share our skills and insights on the climb. It is the Bible which provides the actual terrain we will cover. A guide such as this book, however, can be of help in pointing out trails and pitfalls, many of which have been marked by others who have climbed before us. There will be hard work involved as we clear away the underbrush of introductory problems, questions concerning vocabulary, and cross-references; but it is hoped that, if we persevere, we will

3

break through to vantage points from which insights into God's truths will provide new and wider views of the surrounding countryside, the homes, shops, and fields in which we live and work.

WHY STUDY THE BIBLE?

Let us begin by asking why one should invest time in studying the Bible.

1. Any body of literature or thought which has deeply influenced our national heritage, culture, and literature can hardly be ignored. Certainly the Bible has been such an influence. At a recent gathering someone used the expression, "There's nothing new under the sun" (Eccles. 1:9). Another person in the group, who held several university degrees, replied, "Yes, that comes from Shakespeare, doesn't it?" In spite of his degrees, that person's education was the poorer for not having included a thoughtful study of the Book of Ecclesiastes. Other popular expressions such as "the skin of my teeth," "good Samaritan," "a prodigal," "pharisaic," "the patience of Job," "doubting Thomas," "old as Methuselah," and hundreds more draw meaning from their source, the Bible. Whether one reads the Mayflower Compact, Milton's *Paradise Lost*, the works of Melville or Hawthorne, Thomas Mann's *Joseph* tetralogy, or Faulkner's *Absalom, Absalom!*, a knowledge of the parts of the Bible which the authors had in mind is vital to genuine understanding. A Jewish scholar, Dr. Solomon Goldman, filled 600 pages listing "Echoes and Allusions" to the

Book of Genesis found in European and American literature![1] No person in our culture can truly call himself well educated if he has not made a serious study of the Bible.

Why study the Bible? We all need to study the Bible in order to understand properly our national heritage, culture, and literature. The Christian needs to study the Bible in order to rediscover the reason for his being a Christian and to make contact with the motive-power that created his "family of faith" and prospers its mission in the world.

2. The open Bible is a unique channel of inspiration and motivation at the very heart of the Christian movement.

In A.D. 303 the Roman Emperor Diocletian sought to suppress the young Christian church. One of his first acts was to issue an edict that all Christian Scriptures be burned. His concern was not that the Scriptures were part of the general education of Christians but that they were in fact a unique source of inspiration and power for the church. Diocletian saw the Scriptures to be so vital to the Christian movement that he believed one way to stop the church from undermining Rome's religion, emphasizing emperor worship, was to deprive the Christians of these writings. Even an enemy of the church recognized the truth which later led Tyndale to give up his life in order to provide a Bible in English and caused the paralyzed missionary, Martin Schereschewsky, to type

---

[1] Solomon Goldman, *The Book of Human Destiny*, Vol. II (New York: Harper & Bros., 1948).

out the Bible in Mandarin with a single finger for the Chinese.

The church continually turns to the Bible to find its reason for being, as well as to find the will to strive and the power to become what it ought to be.

For the Christian, the Bible is a collection of writings from the members of his very own family, the "household of faith" (Gal. 6:10), recounting for him the unique history of his family, its sources of inspiration and wealth, and what it means to live up to the family name.

3. Finally, closely related to the Bible's vital role in the life of the Christian movement as a whole is its record of speaking directly and forcefully to individuals. No one ought to ignore a book that has spoken specifically to the needs of so many individuals and changed the direction of so many lives.

About the time the Roman Empire was disintegrating, a brilliant young man named Augustine, disappointed in his search for meaning through the many philosophies of the day, chanced to open a Bible to Romans 13:14. The words ". . . put ye on the Lord Jesus Christ, and make not provision for the flesh . . ." gave a new unity to Augustine's entire life and led him to become a great theologian and African bishop.[1] Over 800 years later a rather self-indulgent reveler in the town of Assisi heard the words of Matthew 10:7-10 read in a worship service: "Heal the sick, raise the dead. . . . You received without pay,

---

[1] Thomas Kepler, "Augustine," *A Journey with the Saints* (Cleveland: World Publishing Co., n.d.), p. 21.

give without pay. Take no gold, nor silver . . . ." Another life was changed and given direction and the Franciscan order, dedicated to humble service, was soon launched. In the sixteenth century a troubled and unsatisfied Augustinian monk was forced to examine Paul's letters in order to prepare some lectures. While studying Romans 1:17 Martin Luther was led to discard his previous attempts to *earn* God's love, and began to preach "justification by faith alone," ushering in the Reformation.[1]

Many reading this book could add to the record of individual lives changed in direction and unified in purpose through confrontation with the Bible.

WHY STUDY JAMES AND I PETER?

Of course all of the above reasons help us to answer the question, "Why study James and I Peter?" since James and I Peter are parts of the Bible. In fact, the authors of James and I Peter do not boast unique views or independent ideas: they present and confirm the views of the leaders of the early Christian church. They are dependent upon the preaching and instruction common to the community of faith, their aim being to apply the mainstream of Christian teaching to the needs of their readers. Our study, therefore, deals not with two isolated writings, but with a representative body of material which brings us into

---

[1] Rudolf Thiel, *Luther*, translated by Gustav Wiencke (Philadelphia: Fortress Press, n.d.), p. 128.

7

deeper understanding of the wider world of biblical thought.

What are the special reasons for singling out James and I Peter for study by contemporary Christians?

For one thing, James and I Peter are brief and outspoken. Because they are brief, we can more easily concentrate our attention and energies on what they have to say; because they are outspoken, we shall find it difficult to obscure or evade the major points they seek to make. This study should help us to appropriate personally outspoken calls to our obedience uttered here and in other biblical books whose message may be less direct and less obvious. This should initiate us into the study of longer and more complicated biblical books.

There may, however, be a special reason for studying the Book of James at just this time in history.

In Luther's day many persons were deeply disturbed by the question, "How can I make myself acceptable to God?" Many tried accumulating all the good deeds they could in order to force God to reward them with his love and favor. Facing a people with this distorted view of Christianity, Luther emphasized the Books of Romans and Galatians which point out that God's love comes freely and is not purchased by good works. Because the Book of James emphasizes good works rather than God's freely given love, Luther did not find in it the message most needful for *his* day, and so could speak of James as an "epistle of straw."

But what is the emphasis needed in our day? Our culture is hardly preoccupied with amassing good deeds or with the question, "How can I make myself acceptable to God?" Our culture seems to take for granted God's stamp of approval on our nation, our family, our preoccupation with material success, and our denominational church life. We, as Americans, tend to believe that we have accumulated too many good deeds—we are too benevolent in our national and church give-away programs. Could it be that the day has come when the "epistle of straw" has come into its own and holds the very emphasis needful for our society? Every parent knows that children go through phases and that a parent must emphasize first one thing and then another to balance the growing child's often one-sided notions and interests if his life is to keep a proper perspective. Perhaps we of the twentieth century have distorted the whole Christian perspective by taking for granted the lesson of God's freely given love and omitting the balancing factor: *God's love transforms those he loves into thankful and obedient servants whose chief purpose in life is to worship him and do works of love, unselfishness, and mercy in the world.* For us the "epistle of straw" may be an "epistle of rock" meant to shatter the comfortable illusion of a discipleship which makes no sacrificial claims upon our time, budget, attitudes, or behavior. James fairly shouts to our age: "Do you want to be shown, you foolish [people], that faith apart from works is barren?" (James 2:20.)

Let us then read James as a letter written directly to us, speaking to our own personal failings. Let James tell us how our foolishness has led to an age in which belief and behavior seem to have little relationship to each other; let James tell us why Christians

9

in our day can seldom be distinguished from non-Christians in the great moral conflicts and the little personal dishonesties of daily life; *let James call us back to a life of obedience, a discipleship that means something and costs something.*

Why study I Peter along with James? First, because it immediately follows James in the Bible and belongs to the same grouping of New Testament letters—the Catholic Epistles.

Second, while James paints in brilliant—even strident—colors the message needful for our day, I Peter provides a perfect background for that message. I Peter takes us back to the very foundation of our faith, exploring the questions, Just what is the Christian community? or What does it mean to be a Christian? In order to answer these questions I Peter asks us to examine the meaning of the sacrament by which we became Christians, the sacrament of baptism: "Baptism . . . now saves you . . ." (I Pet. 3:21).

James calls the disciple to "Christian doing"; I Peter reminds us that "Christian doing" takes place where there is "Christian being."

WHAT IS THE PLACE OF JAMES AND I PETER IN THE BIBLE?

James and I Peter are two early Christian letters (perhaps sermons or essays) in that collection of writings known as the New Covenant or New Testament.

The earliest Christians were a part of Judaism, and

quite naturally accepted the Hebrew Scriptures, the history of God's covenant with Israel, as their Bible. However, to the account of this old covenant with Israel, the Christians soon began to add several writings of their own telling of God's new covenant [1] or new testament with his people through Jesus Christ. After much debate [2] the early church settled upon twenty-seven first- and early second-century writings as the "New Covenant."

First, there are four separate writings called *Gospels*, each of which records certain important events in the life of Jesus in an attempt to convince the reader that Jesus is the "Messiah," the "Son of God."

Then comes The Acts of the Apostles, a continuation of Luke's Gospel. In Acts, Luke goes on to tell how the risen and ascended Jesus continues to lead his church through the Holy Spirit and, by means of inspired men like Paul, to bring the gospel of God's saving grace even to the capital of the Roman Empire itself.

Next are *thirteen letters addressed by Paul to certain of his churches* and to certain individuals. These letters, Romans to Philemon, are probably the earliest writing in the New Testament (about A.D. 50-60) and

---

[1] "Covenant" is an important word in the Bible, having a deeper meaning than simply "agreement." See "Covenant," *The Interpreter's Dictionary of the Bible*, Vol. I, pp. 717-18, 722-23. Also *Genesis: Beginnings of the Biblical Drama* by Charles F. Kraft (Cincinnati: Service Center, 1964), pp. 85-88, 119-27.

[2] For an understanding of how writings came to be gathered to form the Bible, see *The Interpreter's Dictionary of the Bible*'s article on "Canon," Vol. I. pp. 498-532, 524-25.

affirm the meaning of Christianity in the face of local church problems and conflicts. Three of these, I and II Timothy and Titus, are called the Pastoral Letters because they give advice to church leaders concerning pastoral responsibilities; these three letters may contain material by Christian writers later than Paul.

Hebrews follows Paul's letters because Paul was once considered its author. Most scholars would agree today that it is the work of an anonymous Christian.

Following Hebrews, and coming just before the final book of the New Testament, The Revelation to John, is a group of seven brief letters called the *Catholic Epistles* or the *General Letters*. James and I Peter are the first two letters of this group. These letters are called catholic (universal) or general because they were not addressed to the problems of one specific church, as were Paul's letters to Corinth and Colossae, but rather were letters which spoke to the church at large and were to be circulated among many churches.[1]

Although the authors of James and I Peter would no doubt be awed by the fact that their brief writings were being studied 1800 years after they were written and in a language not in existence in their day, it is appropriate that these two Christian letters, meant to be widely read by the churches, should present their message for our guidance and instruction today.

---

[1] It is true, however, that III John, addressed to a specific individual, and perhaps II John, do not technically qualify as "catholic" or "general" letters.

HOW SHOULD WE STUDY
JAMES AND I PETER?

First, James and I Peter should be read through. Just as on a mountain-climbing expedition no one, not even the expedition's guide, can do the climbing for another, so in Bible study no one can do the work of actually covering the chosen terrain—in this case reading James and I Peter—except the individual student.

There are no secret formulas for Bible reading, no substitutes for genuine interest, common sense, and hard work. A few hints, however, may be helpful:

A clear and accurate translation of the Bible should be used. The Revised Standard Version (RSV) will be most convenient since that is the translation most often quoted in this book.

A brief book, such as James, should be read through without interruption. One should be able to read James thoughtfully in less than half an hour.

Once the reading is finished, general impressions may be recorded. Ask yourself: What struck me about the book? Then introductory questions, which should be asked of any biblical book, may be considered: Does the book itself tell me anything about the author and his location in time and place? about his intended readers and their location? about his purpose in writing to them?

Reread James as often as you can, attempting to relate it to the New Testament message as a whole, sometimes searching it for the answer to a particular question that interests you. For example, I Corinthians, chapter 13, emphasizes "love" as the leading prerequisite of a Christian life. Ask yourself: Does James agree with this emphasis of Paul upon Christian love? Does James give first place to some other quality? You may wish to read the Sermon on the Mount (Matthew, chapters 5 through 7); then search James to find similarities or differences. What is their meaning?

There are problems facing your own church and your own life. As you read James, note whether the counsels he addresses to Christians in his local church contain some pointed word or underlying attitude applicable to your need or the need of your local church.

Just as in the first century these New Testament letters were sent to be read before an entire congregation or even to be circulated for hearing and discussion, so in our day, also, biblical books are not meant to be interpreted by individuals in isolation but by Christians in fellowship with one another. Your own understanding of James' letter will become much richer if you study it as a member of a Bible study group in which each member is given the opportunity to state his understanding of the meaning of particular passages and to exchange and discuss with fellow students the various views presented. If you engage in this study alone, read a passage to your family and ask for their impressions; carry your interpretation and questions to a neighbor, your pastor or, at the very least, join in active dialogue with the interpretation presented in this book.

Having read James and I Peter, the reader should then go on to employ whatever special tools for further Bible study are available. No person alone can exhaust them all. Here again cooperation will help: one person can look up the meaning of a puzzling word, another check the use of a key word in other biblical books, and a third can read about practices in the early Christian community which may clarify a given passage.

Here are a few of the tools for Bible study that may be especially helpful:

Your own Bible and your knowledge of it is the most useful tool in the study of any book of the Bible. As we have already noted, James and I Peter are not to be studied in isolation, but rather as books whose emphases are best understood when seen in relation to the rest of the Bible. Does a word or passage puzzle you? Can you think of passages in other biblical books which use the same key words and may clarify the puzzling passage? Your own Bible may provide special help through cross-references and perhaps introductions and notes.

The comparison of a number of *different translations* is valuable, since the New Testament was originally written in Greek, not English, and no single English translation is likely to express every passage of the original in the most accurate and most meaningful way for you. Comparison of the Revised Standard and the King James versions with *The New English Bible,* and the Moffatt, Goodspeed, or Phillips translations of a difficult passage will help direct you to its original meaning. (See "Books for Further Reading," pp. 167 f.)

A complete Bible concordance lists each word occurring in the Bible, giving every verse in which that word is used. This tool requires effort to use, but can be especially rewarding. You may be puzzled, for instance, by the way James uses the word "temptation." A concordance (perhaps even a small one in the back of your own Bible) will show you how the word "temptation" is used elsewhere in the Bible, perhaps indicating that the word "temptation" has several shades of meaning which vary according to the context in which it is used.

A *Bible dictionary* generally presents a brief essay defining or giving the history of each of the persons, places, and key words of the Bible. Looking up the word "James," one will find not only a scholarly discussion of the date, authorship, and purpose of the Book of James, but also a few words concerning each of the persons named James mentioned by the Bible. The new four-volume *Interpreter's Dictionary of the Bible* is available in many public libraries and would be of great help in every church library. (See also pp. 167-170.)

Bible commentaries vary greatly in size and quality. Their purpose is to follow the text of a given book of the Bible verse by verse, commenting on the meaning and significance of each passage, and clarifying difficult words and puzzling references. One of the most helpful works of this kind is the twelve-volume *Interpreter's Bible,* the final volume of which includes commentaries on James and I Peter. It is available in many public and some church libraries. Smaller commentaries written especially for the layman are available (see pp. 167-69). The interested Bible student might well begin collecting commentaries on some of the most important books of the Bible.

Such books as a Bible atlas, volumes depicting life in Bible times, histories of the early church, and writings of the early church fathers will be helpful.

Working with these tools designed to clarify words and determine the author's original intention is only a means and not an end in Bible study for the Christian. There is one more step the Christian reader must take.

Søren Kierkegaard, a Danish Christian of the nineteenth century, explained it thus: Suppose a young man's beloved is of another nationality than he, and writes him a letter in her language, which he cannot understand. What does the young man do? He gets dictionaries and grammar books and works hard to translate that letter into language he can understand. After having done this preliminary work, the young man takes the next step without which all his work would be meaningless: he now fastens all his attention on just what the letter says to *him*, personally: What does his beloved tell him and require of him?

Our reference materials should help to make writings of another age and another culture more understandable to us. But once we have finished with our tools, we should take the important step and ask: What does this Scripture say to *me*, personally? What does it tell me and require of me? What can the author, so close to the event we hold to be crucial in world history, relate concerning that event and its meaning for my existence? What is this early member of my family, the "household of faith," telling me about my origins and the family's reason for being? No commentary, concordance, or studyguide can take this final step for the reader. But real Bible study requires this personal encounter.

How is this book to help in our study of James and I Peter? It is hoped that this introductory chapter has oriented us for the study ahead, reminding us of the basic reasons for embarking upon such a study and giving a few hints concerning ways of studying the Bible.

Beginning with Chapter 2, a passage-by-passage commentary is provided to guide the reader through James and I Peter. After reading James, follow the text of James and of this commentary together, allowing the commentary to stimulate your own reading and interpretation of James. Later, follow the same procedure with I Peter. The commentary, although it is based upon many readings of James and I Peter, a study of the Greek text, and a reading of the works of many scholars, will not have all the answers. Question the commentary; discuss its interpretations and your own with other persons. It is in such encounters that we begin to lose our self-consciousness and become aware of a truth beyond ourselves.

You will note that the commentary in Chapters 2 through 5 reproduces a large part of the text of James and I Peter. These passages should recall to your mind the impressions you have already gained and the meanings you have already found, allowing you to enter into an active conversation with the writer and with one another.

Thomas Jefferson did not approve of everything to

be found in the New Testament. He therefore set to work with scissors and paste, clipped out only those passages he found to be personally meaningful, and created his own abbreviated New Testament.[1] We may not agree with Jefferson's high-handed manner of dealing with the Bible, but, in a sense, almost every one of us has done something similar. Our personal Bible can honestly claim to contain only those books or passages we have taken the time to study and to apply to our lives. It is our hope that this study commentary will aid in adding the often neglected Books of James and I Peter to the personal Bibles of many readers.

---

[1] *The Jefferson Bible:* The life and morals of Jesus of Nazareth, extracted from the Gospels, together with a comparison of his doctrines with those of others. By Thomas Jefferson. (New York: Thompson Publishing Co., 1902.)

2

Commentary
on James
Chapter 1

THE LETTER OF JAMES

Let us begin our commentary by examining the title of this twentieth book of the New Testament: The Letter (or Epistle) of James. Is this title accurate? Was the Book of James originally written as a letter? If not, what was its original form?

First, we should remember that the Book of James probably had no title when first written. The first verse provided the only identification considered necessary. Second, although the first verse of James

---

NOTE: Words quoted directly from the Books of James and I Peter are printed in boldface.

follows the form common to Greek letters of that day, the writing proceeds without any further evidence that the book is, in fact, an epistle. Moreover it ends in a surprisingly abrupt manner, omitting the words generally closing a genuine letter (see James 5:19-20). This has led some scholars to suggest that James was not originally a letter at all, but an early Christian sermon or essay which was copied, given a letter-like salutation, and circulated among the churches for their edification.

Other scholars point out that James' manner of presenting ethical demands resembles that of the popular moral discourses (or diatribes) of certain Greek philosophers, or perhaps copies the form of instruction given in Jewish synagogues to pagan converts. Still other scholars believe that, if just a few words are omitted (in 1:1 and 2:1), James becomes a completely Jewish rather than a Christian writing. They suggest that some early Christian simply revised a Jewish writing, perhaps one telling the story of Jacob's [1] blessing of the twelve tribes (see Genesis, chapter 49), transforming it into a Christian document.

Determining the original literary form of the Book of James is not simply a scholarly game. Knowing whether it was first an actual letter or an early Christian sermon, or whether it copied Greek or Jewish moral discourses, can help us to understand many of the things its author says.

---

[1] "James" is a form of the name Jacob-Jacobus; an English equivalent for the Greek word for "Jacob."

What then was the original form of James? This you must seek to determine as you reread, study, and compare James with other writings. To date, there is no one generally accepted answer.

To this writer, the author of James seems to be an early Christian teacher who felt a close kinship to the Jewish Wisdom writers. He understood himself to be in the same tradition as the writers of Proverbs in the Old Testament or Ecclesiasticus (also called the Wisdom of Jesus the Son of Sirach) in the Apocrypha.[1] Perhaps we could picture James as a religious Jew living among pagans, acquainted with Greek language and learning, who heard the good news of the Messiah's coming and became a Christian. His own background led him to become a respected teacher in the church. In his day, however, perhaps the late first or early second century, the teacher saw many pagan converts entering the church whose moral standards were far below those of the earlier Jewish converts. Besides this, many earlier converts were departing from their original high calling and were now allowing prejudices, gossiping, and squabbles to multiply in the life of the congregations.

Rising to this moral crisis, the teacher drew upon his heritage of Jewish Wisdom literature and the early ethical codes taking shape in the Christian community, and penned *a Christian Wisdom book calling believers to a moral revival*. Gathering wise sayings

---

[1] The Apocrypha proper is a collection of Jewish books found in the Roman Catholic and Eastern Orthodox Bible but generally omitted from the Protestant Bible.

concerning the obedient life from the new community's instructions to converts, from remembrances of Jesus' commands, and from the laws of Judaism, *the teacher wrote a tract which sought to guide the unsteady or immature converts toward Christian perfection or maturity.*

Is such a scroll, if written in the situation described, of value today?

Sharp words concerning *Christian doing* were necessary in the teacher's day and apparently have been necessary in the church ever since. The teacher lived during a moral crisis in the life of his church and a similar critical situation faces the church in our own day. If we claim a place in that same family of faith to which the teacher belonged and detect in our behavior as Christians some unsteadiness or immaturity, then *the teacher's sharp words and call to Christian maturity are addressed to us.*

1:1 James, a servant of God and of the Lord Jesus Christ, to the twelve tribes in the dispersion: Greeting.

Here we begin the Book of James itself, and its beginning is a salutation. Greek letters of the first century commonly opened this way, giving: (1) the sender's name, (2) the identification of those to whom he wrote, and (3) the Greek word *chairein,* which we translate "greeting." Let us examine these three parts of the salutation:

1. James, a servant of God and of the Lord Jesus Christ.

The sender identifies himself by this single phrase. The word "servant" which occurs so often in the New Testament is the Greek word *doulos* and means an owned household servant—a "slave." [1] It is the word Jesus applied to his own ministry and used to define the task of his followers (Matt. 20:26-28).[2] "Slave" of God could be applied to Moses (Rev. 15:3), to Christian leaders (Titus 1:1), or to any Christian (I Peter 2:16). Paul develops this biblical picture to describe Christians as household "slaves" whom God graciously "adopts" as "sons" (Gal. 4:1-7).

Do *we* not identify *ourselves* in this day and age more often by what we own than by that to which we owe our allegiance? "I'm the one who owns the house up the block." "He's the one with the blue convertible." "They're the ones who own half the town." But what *owns us?* James' self-description might mark him in our day as a dangerous religious fanatic, for we seldom think in terms of a positive captivity. We rather automatically assume that the consequences of captivity—slavery—must be negative. We add to the word "slave" the phrases "of drink," "of drugs," "of sex." The New Testament affirms that these lesser captivities are perversions which creep in when the one needful allegiance which unifies all life is absent, for all of us need to be "owned" by something larger than ourselves.

---

[1] Note that the RSV sometimes adds a footnote reminding the reader that "servant" can also be translated "slave." See John 15:20, for example.

[2] *The Revised Standard Version, The New English Bible,* and Phillips' translation all use the word "slave" in this verse.

24

James is the slave of whom? He unites the old Testament phrase slave of God with the new community's slave of the Lord Jesus Christ, witnessing to the historic tie recognized between God's dealing with Israel and with his church, the new Israel.

The title Lord (*kurios* in Greek) indicates here a "slave owner," for the Christian acknowledges that he has been "purchased" and is owned by his Lord, Jesus Christ. When angry Roman officials demanded that Christians accused of disloyalty repeat the traditional words, *kurios Kaisar* (Lord Caesar), many Christians declared their allegiance to Christ and risked their lives by using instead the words *kurios Christos* (Lord Christ). The use of the term Lord in this phrase signifies the Christian's total commitment; the use of the word Jesus implies his conviction that God fully expressed his Lordship in the person of a flesh-and-blood Galilean; and the addition of the word Christ (Messiah or anointed) bears witness to the Christian belief that God's promise of a Messiah to Israel had been fulfilled in the person of his Son.

Thus James has told us in his first sentence that he owes total allegiance to Jesus whom he acknowledges as the promised Messiah.

But does the personal name James tell us anything more about the author? Actually there are several persons named James mentioned in the New Testament. *James* the brother of John and son of Zebedee (Mark 3:17) and *James* the son of Alphaeus (Mark 3:18) were both disciples of Jesus. Mark 15:40 mentions a "*James* the younger" and Luke 6:16 mentions *James,* father of the disciple Judas (not Judas

Iscariot). Besides these there is *James*, the brother of Jesus, to whom the risen Christ appeared (I Cor. 15:7), who was called a "pillar" of the church (Gal. 2:9), and who presided at the Jerusalem Conference (Acts 15:13-19).

Is one of these men called James the author we seek or is our author some otherwise unknown Christian named James, or is someone simply writing in the name of one of the persons mentioned in the preceding paragraph? Once again there is not enough evidence for us to be certain, and scholars have not come to any agreement.

Here are a few bits of evidence to be weighed when considering the identity of *this* James:

A. The early church was apparently uncertain whether or not to include the Book of James in the New Testament. Our earliest list of New Testament books does not appear to have included the Book of James. Would there have been such hesitancy if an original disciple or the brother of Jesus were the known author?

B. To our knowledge, none of the early church fathers until Origen of Alexandria (middle of the third century) quotes from the Book of James.

C. The historian Eusebius of Caesarea (early fourth century) is of the opinion that the brother of Jesus was the author but considers the epistle a "disputed" book in the church.

D. Its Jewish-moralistic emphasis might indicate that the brother of Jesus was the author; Acts, on the other hand, pictures Jesus' brother as interested in ritual practices (Acts 15:19-21) which are not mentioned in the Book of James.

E. The Book of James is written in excellent popular Greek and quotes from the Greek translation of the Old Testament. Could such a book have been written by any of the biblical persons named James listed above, all of whom were probably Aramaic-speaking?

F. If Jesus' brother or an original disciple was the author, why does he not say so, and why does he not have more (some would say "anything") to say about Jesus' life?

Across the centuries the traditional theory has been that James the Just, brother of Jesus and leader of the early Jerusalem church, authored the Book of James. Many scholars doubt that theory, however, suggesting that either an otherwise unknown teacher named James or someone simply writing in the name of James the Just wrote the scroll. A few scholars make a compromise, suggesting that a Jerusalem sermon or the teachings of Jesus' brother were later added to and translated into Greek to form the present Book of James. If the brother of Jesus did write the book, it may be the earliest book of the New Testament, dating possibly as early as A.D. 49. If someone else authored the book, it might be one of the latest written books of the Bible, its date perhaps being as late as A.D. 150.

It has no doubt become obvious to the reader that if one hopes to obtain definite authentication of the book's authorship through biblical scholarship, one is bound to be disappointed. Our uncertainty regarding the identity of "James," however, should be kept in perspective. In some quarters one can spark a major debate with the question, "Who wrote Shakespeare's plays?" and these plays are of relatively recent origin. Likewise, historical and literary experts not only debate whether Homer actually wrote the *Iliad* and *Odyssey*, but go so far as to question whether Homer ever actually existed! It is well to inquire seriously concerning an author's identity, but the *value* of a work should not be judged by whether or not one succeeds in identifying the author. The teacher who wrote the Book of James would no doubt be deeply disturbed if he thought that his readers' attention was focused upon his identity rather than on what was obviously of most importance to him: his message.

2. To the twelve tribes in the dispersion.

The second part of the salutation names those to whom the letter is written. According to biblical tradition, the Hebrew nation was composed of twelve tribes, while the dispersion refers to the "scattering" of the Hebrew tribes among all the pagan nations through warfare, captivity, and emigration.

Does this mean that James is therefore addressed to Jews rather than to Christians? No. The earliest Christians accepted the Jewish Scriptures as their own, attended the Jewish temple (Acts 2:46), preached in the synagogues (Acts 9:20; 13:5), and called themselves "the Israel of God" (Gal. 6:16). God had made those Jews (and soon Gentiles also)

28

who accepted Jesus as Messiah the true heirs of the twelve tribes. Any Christian reading the scroll of James knew he was being addressed, for the joys and responsibilities of God's "chosen people" were now his. This new Israel knew itself to be even more of a dispersion than did old Israel, for Christians were soon intermingled as leaven in the measure of every ancient city, yet had no land to call their own. Christians were pilgrims, "aliens and exiles" (I Pet. 2:11), humbly serving their Lord in a world order they could never call home. "Our commonwealth is in heaven," wrote Paul to the Philippians (3:20).

Does the church still take seriously its Judaistic heritage and its responsibilities as a "chosen people"? Even more to the point, are Christians still recognizable as "aliens and exiles" who are dispersed throughout the world to serve, and who refuse to be conformed to this world's order? In a later chapter we will see that I Peter raises even more pointedly the question of what it means to be a pilgrim people.

3. Greeting.

This salutation, commonly found in Greek letters of that day, occurs in two other letters in the New Testament, the letter of Claudius Lysias to Felix (Acts 23:26) and the letter associated with James, brother of Jesus, which carried the Jerusalem Conference decrees to Gentile converts (Acts 15:23).

The basic meaning of the Greek word *chairein* (translated "greeting," and akin to our word "cheer") is "rejoice" rather than simply "greeting," and the author may be playing upon this basic meaning when he begins the next verse, "Count it all joy . . . ."

1:2-4　²Count it all joy, my brethren, when you meet various trials . . . . ³testing . . . produces steadfastness . . . ⁴that you may be perfect and complete, lacking in nothing.

We come now to the body of this "Christian Wisdom Book." The teacher issues his call to a life of mature discipleship in a time of moral crisis.

The family of believers, the brethren, are to look upon trials as all joy. This is not ordinary. Usually we think of trials as nuisances, accidents, or horrible experiences. Disciples, however, like their Lord, are to have an extraordinary way of looking at things. They are to see persecution as a blessing (Matt. 5:10-12), self-denial as a way of life (Mark 8:34), and the losing of life as a way of gaining it (Mark 8:35). The popular picture of success is the aggressive go-getter who makes a comfortable place for himself; the disciple's picture of success is the meek and merciful peacemaker who denies himself and suffers for righteousness' sake (Matt. 5:5-11).

Why does James begin by speaking of trials?

Could James be writing to Christians at a specific time of persecution? The Book of Revelation and possibly I Peter were written in times of persecution but it seems likely that the term trials in James should be understood in a more general sense.

Trials were a special concern in the church from its

beginning. Believers were often poor folk in adversity, and to their habitual trials were soon added the anger of Jews, the cruelty of pagan mobs, and the harsh justice of the Roman law. It is likely that the catechism or instruction for new converts in the early church included a special section on the meaning of trials and the proper behavior for a Christian in times of difficulty. Such training regarding trials was prompted by a practical necessity not unlike that which has led the leaders of sit-in demonstrators and voter registration workers in our own day to institute courses for their followers on "taking abuse" properly.

That a regular pattern did develop for instructing Christians concerning trials can be seen by comparing James 1:2-4 with Romans 5:3-5 ("we rejoice in our sufferings") and I Peter 1:6 7 ("you rejoice . . . though you suffer"). Luke 6:22 makes it clear that the church believed that, in formulating its catechism, it was following the injunction of Christ himself: "Blessed are you when men hate you . . . exclude you . . . revile you . . . cast out your name. . . . Rejoice . . . leap for joy . . . your reward is in heaven."

James chose to begin his tract for bolstering unsteady Christians by borrowing from this "basic training manual" which prepared Christians for "front-line service." Apparently he observed that many believers of his day had become "sunshine Christians" whose faith was eclipsed by the first clouds of adversity. James believed that trials ought to purge and purify one's faith rather than dilute faith and make it ineffectual. He would have preferred "foxhole religion," wherein one turns to God in time of trial, to "sunshine religion" wherein one worships God only when life's sky is cloudless.

Why are trials *to be counted as* joy?

Trials are to be counted as joy not because they are good in themselves. That trials are a part of every life is simply an honest observation, but the teacher does not advocate going in search of them. Only masochists who enjoy punishing themselves or the proud who wish to show off their own powers consciously seek out trials or temptations. Actually the word used in James 1:2 and translated in the Revised Standard Version as trials is the Greek word *peirasmois* which connotes both external difficulties and inner impulses to sin. It is the word which Christ used in the Lord's Prayer, where it is translated as "temptation." "Lead us not into temptation." We might therefore say that the Christian is to pray to be delivered from trials just as Christ himself prayed in Gethsemane: ". . . if thou art willing, remove this cup from me" (Luke 22:42). Although the Christian is not to search for trials, when they come he is to count them as joy because they can work for good in the Christian life. Trials are a rugged part of the obstacle course through which the testing of one's faith is experienced. This testing builds up the Christian athlete's steadfastness (fortitude); and the goal of the course he runs is the perfect, complete, or mature life of discipleship.

What is the secret of counting trials *as* joy?

Dr. Victor Frankl tells of a husband who came to his clinic despairing of life itself because his wife had died. Dr. Frankl asked the husband what it would have been like for his wife if she had survived him. The man admitted that his wife had been a sensitive person who could not have borne her loss and loneliness. So, Frankl pointed out, the husband himself was bearing the suffering and loneliness which might have been the wife's lot. This realization made the husband's own suffering become meaningful to him and it began to discipline rather than to destroy him.[1]

The secret of counting trials as joy is in finding *meaning* in one's difficulties. James makes it clear that for the Christian trials can always be meaningful, for they put to the test one's faith and provide a route—through increasing steadfastness, or fortitude—to perfect and complete discipleship.

James has not said all that the Bible can say about joy gained through trials. A study of the word joy with the help of a concordance or Bible dictionary, for example, will reveal that joy was especially associated with God's restoring of his people (Isa. 52:8-9) and hence with the events which would usher in a new age (Matt. 2:10; Luke 24:52). The coming of this new age or new kingdom could be pictured as a birth, the birth of a new world order, accompanied by the birth pains caused by the reactionary forces and vested interests of the old age as it struggled in panic to avoid being superseded by the new order of love and those who practiced it. Christians saw themselves as the heralds of the new age, and so

---

[1] Victor Frankl, *Man's Search for Meaning* (New York: Washington Square Press, 1964), pp. 178-79.

whatever suffering came through their witnessing to the new kingdom of love was a special joy, for they were sharing in the birth pangs of the new kingdom which was coming into being. Here then is the special biblical sense in which trials are to be counted as joy. When believers dare to live according to the new order of love, selflessness, and brotherhood, and suffer suspicion and hatred on this account, they share in the sufferings of Christ and have a part in the birth of the new age.

1:5-8 ⁵If any of you lacks wisdom, let him ask God who gives to all men generously and without reproaching, . . .

This is an appropriate place to pause and ask the reader whether his reading of James has revealed any underlying theme which gives unity to the whole writing. Is there a basic thought pattern of the author or a developing outline which gives structure to the Book of James?

Some have said, "James seems to jump from one thing to another without any plan. The book is just a jumble of dozens of subjects." If this is also your opinion, you can find scholars who will agree with you. B. S. Easton, in *The Interpreter's Bible,* asserts that the Book of James has "no 'general theme' at all" and "lacks any formal plan," [1] while W. E. Oesterley observes that most commentators agree that James is

---

[1] B. S. Easton, "The Epistle of James: Introduction," *The Interpreter's Bible* (Nashville: Abingdon Press, 1957), Vol. XII, pp. 3, 4.

a collection of "unconnected sayings."[1] Once again, however, there is sharp disagreement among scholars. A. T. Cadoux writes: "It is strange that so many writers have found [James] formless, for it is probably the most patterned Book in the Bible."[2] What is one to believe? Does James have an underlying theme, structure, and unity, or does it not? Once again the reader must make his own decision through reading and rereading the Book of James, attempting to enter the mind of the author and to reason with him from one passage to the next.

This writer is inclined to believe that the more one reads James, the more one comes to see an underlying structure and unity in the book. Certainly this unity is not perfect, for James (like the Book of Proverbs) is an anthology of "wisdom" and thus at times seems to be no more than a miscellany of wise sayings and advice. But the author does seem to have a major theme which answers the moral crisis of his day: *believers must grow up to perfect and complete discipleship, and this Christian maturity must show itself in Christian doing.* Besides this primary call to mature and active discipleship, the author has various subthemes or special interests. For example, he believes the church needs special instruction concerning the *meaning of trials or temptations,* the *place of the rich and the poor,* and the *use of the tongue.* The Book of James may well remind one of a great piece

[1] W. E. Oesterley, *The Expositor's Greek Testament* (London: Hodder and Stoughton, n.d.), Vol. IV, p. 407.
[2] A. T. Cadoux, *The Thought of St. James* (London: James Clarke and Co., Ltd., 1944), p. 6.

of music as it sounds its dominant and subordinate themes, repeats them in slightly different forms, and intertwines one theme with another.

Besides finding a major theme and subthemes, the perceptive reader can discover a number of connecting links which lead James from one topic to another. Watch to see how a word introduced in one verse is picked up again for special comment in a following verse or how a question which is raised by one passage is then singled out and answered by a following passage. These connections are often subtle, but a genuine study reveals a surprising number of them.

Now let us apply what we have said to the passage at hand, James 1:5-8. One scholar declares that there is "no thought connection" between this passage and what has gone before.[1] Is this really so? The previous passage exhorts the believer to become perfect, complete, lacking in nothing. An unsteady Christian might then well ask: But I am not perfect and complete. What can I do if I lack what is necessary for mature discipleship? James seems to assume such a question will be asked and therefore continues, If any of you lacks wisdom, let him ask God who gives to all . . . . We must remember that for a Wisdom writer the word "wisdom" meant not simply a single gift or characteristic but one's whole attitude of life, one's knowledge of God's law, and one's willingness to be obedient to it. James is saying, "If trials have not caused you to grow up in discipleship as they should,

---

[1] W. E. Oesterley, *The Expositor's Greek Testament*, Vol. IV, p. 422.

then you must turn to God and ask him to make known to you the way of discipleship and to provide the strength for you to follow that way" (cf. Matt. 7:7).

Here, however, an inquiring Christian might raise another question: Does this mean that just anyone can ask God for wisdom and receive it? Once again James seems to assume the question and immediately clarifies: But let him ask in faith. . . . [you] must not suppose that a double-minded man . . . will receive anything . . . . James makes clear that it is the humble petitioner whose only hope is God, not the man of divided loyalties, who receives from the Lord. It is of interest to note that James shares the special aver sion of Wisdom writers to double-mindedness or hypocrisy. Ecclesiasticus, for example, warns: ". . . Do not approach him with a divided mind" (1: 28) and "Woe . . . to . . . the sinner . . . who walks along two ways" (2:12). Later passages in James which stress Christian works must be balanced by this assertion that faith alone is the condition for re- ceiving an answer to one's prayer and hence is basic in the life of the Christian.

Before leaving James 1:5-8, one might mark James' brief but suggestive description of the way in which God gives: to all [who ask in faith], generously, and without reproaching. Did James wish to make clear that God's giving has none of the imperfections which so often spoil human giving? Is it not true that by playing favorites, by giving grudgingly, and by ac- companying gifts with condescending lectures, our own giving has often been spoiled and has fostered hatred rather than love?

1:9-11   ⁹Let the lowly brother boast in his exalta-
tion, ¹⁰and the rich in his humiliation . . . .

Rich and poor are often contrasted in the Bible: "Blessed are you poor . . . woe to you that are rich . . ." (Luke 6:20, 24; cf. Luke 1:52-53). The wealthier we become, the more completely and conveniently we seem to forget the New Testament's terrible warnings concerning riches (Mark 10:25; Luke 12:16-21).

James will return to the subject of rich and poor in 2:1-13 and 5:1-6, and we will examine the topic further then. We must, however, ask what part this first reference to the lowly brother and the rich plays in his discussion. He has already affirmed that God makes available to all men the wisdom necessary for obedient discipleship. Could it be that James now demonstrates this by showing that the two extremes of society, the lowly and the rich, are both dealt with by God in such a way that they are confronted by their dependence upon him? The lowly have nothing to boast of save his attentions to them (cf. James 2:5), while the rich, in spite of their power, are mortal like other men and thus must find their hope in their very weakness—their dependence upon God.

James compares the life of the rich with grass which suddenly withers when the sun rises with its scorching heat. This latter phrase could be more literally translated "the sun rises with the southeasterly wind

—the sirocco" (cf. Hos. 13:15; Ezek. 17:10). The sudden coming of this hot dry wind from the desert is said to turn vegetation from green to brown in a single day in Palestine, an effective picture of the fleetingness of life (cf. Isa. 40:6-8).

1:12 **Blessed is the man who endures trial, for when he has stood the test he will receive the crown of life which God has promised to those who love him.**

Here is a beatitude, a blessing, which calls to mind one of Jesus' own beatitudes (see Matt. 5:11). Following the rules of a good speaker or writer, James is repeating what he has already said in 1:2-4. This beatitude, in fact, summarizes and brings to a climax all that has gone before:

Become perfect and complete disciples:
1. through trials which test faith
2. by God's gift of wisdom in answer to prayer
3. through God's gifts which are for all, lowly and rich.

Climax: Endure trial and receive the crown of life.

The word "crown" in the Greek text is *stephanos* (hence the name "Stephen") and generally refers to the wreath of leaves given a victorious athlete or general after he has come through the trials of a racecourse or battle. Among the Wisdom writers, wisdom itself is sometimes spoken of as a crown or as life (cf. Prov. 1:9, 4:9, 8:35) and James may have this in mind as he parallels perfect and complete, wisdom, and crown of life; all three are ways of describing the goal

39

of discipleship, the gift God offers the faithful. It is significant that the Christian's reward is pictured as a wreath (cf. Rev. 2:10; I Pet. 5:4; II Tim. 4:8). Not only does the use of this term clearly show that the training and discipline of an athlete or soldier are required of the Christian disciple, but it also suggests the special quality of the Christian's reward. The wreath of leaves is worthless in itself, having meaning only as one recognizes the authority of the giver. Likewise, the gift of full life in fellowship with God seems worthless to the mercenary, who serves for material gain, but is priceless to the faithful.

James speaks of the crown . . . which God has promised to those who love him.

The word promised could refer to such promises as those found in Deuteronomy 7:9 ("keeps covenant . . . with those who love him") or Luke 22:30 ("you may . . . sit on thrones . . ."). The words to those who love him also occur in Romans 8:28 (". . . in everything God works for good with those who love him . . ."), and again in James 2:5.[1] This is the first time the word love appears in James, giving a new depth to James' picture of the relationship between Lord and disciple.

1:13-15   [13]Let no one say when he is tempted, "I am tempted by God . . . ."

As has been pointed out, the Greek word *peirasmois* can mean both external trials and internal tempta-

---

[1] Also compare the Wisdom Book, Ecclesiasticus: "He supplied her [Wisdom] to those who love him" (Ecclesiasticus 1:10).

tions. Earlier in James 1:2 the Revised Standard Version of the Bible translated this Greek word as **trials** for it seemed to emphasize external hardships; now various forms of this same Greek word are translated **tempt** and **tempted,** because the emphasis seems to be upon inward desire which entices (or lures) a person to sin.[1]

Having emphasized that God can use trials to test and train his disciples, James now proceeds to answer a question which might arise: Does this mean that God creates external hardship on purpose, or even more unbelievable, does this mean that God creates the internal enticements to evil which humans experience? In a wider sense, this is the age-old question, Who is to blame for the evil in the world?

James ascribes evil to the individual. We are lured and enticed by our own desire, as a fish or animal is lured foolishly by a dangerous bait. (Lured and enticed can both be used in speaking of fishing and hunting in Greek.) Desire yielded to gives birth to sin, and sin incubates until, in its fully-developed form, it brings forth death. Genesis likewise finds the origin of death to be human sin (Gen. 2:17), as does Paul: "The wages of sin is death" (Rom. 6:23); "It was sin working death in me . . ." (Rom. 7:13).

James' words, **Let no one say . . . "I am tempted**

---

[1] The King James Version uses "temptation" in James 1:2 and "tempted" or "tempt" in verses 13-15; *The New English Bible* uses "trials of various kinds" in verse 2 and in verse 13 both "trial" and "temptation." See also *The New Testament in Modern English* by J. B. Phillips which has "trials and temptations" in verses 2 and 12, and "tempt and temptation" in verses 13-15.

by God," probably indicate that there were those in the church who excused their own failings by blaming God. Perhaps James is giving very practical correction to Christians recently converted from paganism who still thought in terms of the Greek and Roman gods. These pagan gods were not above practicing evil and luring humans to evil deeds, as a reading of Homer or the Greek tragedies reveals. Plato himself advised that in the perfect republic young people must not read stories of the immoral actions of the gods. James affirms that there is no evil in the disciples' Lord and that he entices no one to evil.

One of Carl Sandburg's poems takes our own age to task for subtly shrugging off the evils in which we are involved by similarly putting them at God's doorstep: "It is God's will." At the scene of a fire which trapped garment workers in an upper loft from which one girl jumped to her death, the poet pictures someone in the crowd looking at the dead girl and murmuring: "It is the hand of God." The poet responds, "It is the hand of God and the lack of fire escapes." [1] The poet's answer should speak to us of the social sins which result in discrimination against races, in warfare, starving peoples, crowded mental hospitals, ill-equipped juvenile homes, and in corruption in government—all of which we are tempted to shrug off as not our responsibility but simply the way of the world. Isn't it true that God must expect us to

[1] From "Anna Imroth" from *Chicago Poems* by Carl Sandburg. Copyright 1916 by Holt, Rinehart and Winston, Inc. Copyright 1944 by Carl Sandburg. Reprinted by permission of Holt, Rinehart and Winston, Inc.

do our part, to use the minds and hands he has given us, to build the world's fire escapes?

1:16-18 [17] Every good endowment and every perfect
gift is from . . . the Father of lights . . .

The same train of thought continues. Negatively one can say that God does not send down enticement to evil; positively one can say that every good endowment and every perfect gift is from above. These words may have been borrowed by James from some anonymous Greek poet, for in Greek they form a hexameter, a common poetic form.

Still in this poetic vein James, in a beautiful passage, goes on to describe God as the Father of lights with whom there is no variation or shadow due to change. This calls to mind the Genesis account of God's setting the lesser and the greater lights in the firmament.[1] The God who created the stars, moon, and sun can himself be compared to a pure center of illumination which, by its very nature, sends out not darkness but only light (cf. I John 1:5). James may also have had in mind the pagan belief that the heavenly bodies, by their varying positions in the heavens, could rule over man's destinies either for good or for ill (a belief still held by many, for astrology is far from dead). But the Father of lights, who rules over the heavenly bodies, is constant, never varying in position. The heavenly lights themselves may vary from season to season; the moon may wane, the sun may

---

[1] Charles F. Kraft, *Genesis: Beginnings of the Biblical Drama* (Cincinnati: Service Center, 1964), pp. 35-36.

43

set, and mists may put all these lights in shadow, but in God there is no variation or shadow due to change.

This passage continues with one more sentence describing God's power and goodness: of his own will he brought us forth by the word of truth that we should be a kind of first fruits of his creatures.

James probably refers now to that specific proof of God's goodness which is of special interest to his readers: God created the community of believers to usher in a new age. The existence of the church is no accident, but a deliberate act of his own will. God, in a sense, appears in the role of mother to the church: He brought us forth. God is pictured elsewhere as a mother hen protecting her brood (Ps. 36:7), a mother eagle teaching her young to fly (Deut. 32:11), a human mother caring for her children (Isa. 66:13).

The word of truth by which God created the church probably refers specifically to the gospel, the "good news": "the word of truth, the gospel of your salvation" (Eph. 1:13; cf. Mark 4:14, Col. 1:5).

The purpose of this bringing forth, this creation or birth of the church by the gospel, was that we should be a kind of first fruits of his creatures. The first fruits are the earliest figs and olives to ripen, the very first of the grain ready for harvest. These first fruits are the happy signal that the time for the general harvest must be near. Christians are the sign that God's harvest time is dawning; they are the first to mature in God's new age. Moreover, according to the Mosaic law of the Old Testament, the first fruits of fields and orchards were to be taken to the temple and offered to God in thanksgiving as tokens of the whole harvest. Likewise the community of believers must offer itself in service to God on behalf of the whole creation: "For the creation waits with eager longing for the revealing of the sons of God" (Rom. 8:19).

1:19-21 ¹⁹. . . let every man be quick to hear, slow to speak, slow to anger . . . ²¹Put away all filthiness . . . receive with meekness the implanted word . . . .

James has affirmed the goodness of God who answers the prayers of those who ask in faith (1:5), who sends not evil (1:13) but rather every perfect gift (1:17), and creates the community of believers by the word of truth (1:18). His readers may well ask at this point: What then can we do in response to all this goodness of God? Again, James seems to assume such a question.

How should one respond to God's goodness? . . . Be quick to hear, slow to speak, slow to anger, . . . put away . . . filthiness . . . receive with meekness [quiet humility] the . . . word.

What is the sum total of these commands? *The disciple should be receptive and submissive before God.* James is generally pictured as the advocate of a practical and active Christianity. While this is true, it is too often forgotten that he also places special emphasis upon quiet and humble receptivity (receive with meekness). This emphasis is found not only in the present passage but also in his earlier exhortations to endurance and a patient steadfastness or fortitude in time of trials.

The command to put away certain things which do not belong in a Christian life appears many times in the New Testament (I Pet. 2:1; Rom. 13:12; Eph. 4:25) and may have been a regular part of the early Christian catechism for new converts. It may have been customary to give these converts a specific list of the pagan practices described as filthiness and wickedness which must be taken off like old filthy clothes before one puts on the white garment of baptism or the new armor of God (cf. Rom. 13:12).

The admonition to put away what does not belong to a disciple's life is immediately followed by the command to receive . . . the implanted word. This juxtaposition may remind us of Jesus' parable which warns that, if left empty, a house swept clean of evil will simply attract greater evils (cf. Luke 11:24 ff.). Christianity is not simply the weeding out of bad habits; it is the filling of life with positive meaning and purpose contained in God's word which saves. Word is a key term in James, binding verse 18 to our present verse (21) and verse 21 to verse 22:

Verse 18   word of truth which created the church
Verse 21   the implanted word sent by God to save
         the receptive
Verse 22   the word which Christians are not only
         to hear, but to do.

1:22-27   ²²But be doers of the word, and not hearers only, deceiving yourselves.

The word by which the Father created the church, the saving word—the command—which is to be received in meekness, is also the word which requires obedient doing: But be doers of the word. James has emphasized the quiet willingness to listen which is the Christian's proper response to God's goodness. Now he must make clear that this attitude of humble receptivity does not make of Christianity a coffee-break from the hard realities of life, a romantic wandering in the garden alone with Jesus, a meditative philosophy, an aesthetic mood, or even a "great ideas" discussion. The gospel makes of the Christian a doer who acts.

The call to be doers of the word and not hearers only is often seized upon as the very heart of James' message, the command which sums up the whole content of the Book of James. We have already seen, however, that much has gone before this commandment. James has called his hearers to be perfect and complete, to be mature disciples. He has spoken of trials and asking in faith, of the crown of life, of temptations, of God's perfect gifts, and of many other things. Separated from these related sayings, the command to be doers might well be misinterpreted to mean "be busybodies, be a church that hides its emptiness in a confusion of activities, be doing in order to mask your fear of the quiet, of yourself, and of your neighbor." The misinterpretation of the Christian call to be up and doing is no remote danger; to many, Christian doing has come to mean "busy-work."

Is the command, be doers of the word, really the heart of the Book of James? In our opinion, it appears to be not so much the *heart* of James' message as *the life blood which flows from that heart*. The heart of

James' concern is that believers should be perfect and complete, receive the wisdom of Christian maturity, and grow up as disciples. But James found that the church of his day was faced with a dangerous moral crisis. Many Christians were not growing up to mature discipleship. What had stunted their growth? James' diagnosis was that many were attempting to separate belief from morality, faith from works, hearing from doing, and that their discipleship had thus become an empty self-deception.

Having made his diagnosis, James proceeds to hammer at the necessary connection between what one believes and how one acts. *Much of the remainder of his treatise (chapters 2 through 5) is composed of concrete examples of ways in which the church must act out its faith, must do the gospel it has heard.*

In verses 23-25 James compares the hearer who is not a doer to a man who simply glances at his passing appearance in a mirror and goes away forgetting what he saw. The disciple is not to be like this. The disciple is to peer long and hard into that which is eternal, the law of liberty. Because he perseveres in this contact with God's eternal will, the disciple will not forget what he sees but rather will be transformed in his very manner of living; he will be blessed in his doing. In the Gospels, Jesus pronounces a similar blessing on those who put his teachings into practice: " 'If you know these things, blessed are you if you do them' " (John 13:17; cf. Luke 11:28; Matt. 7:24; Rom. 2:13). The law of liberty in which the disciple is to persevere probably refers to the Ten Commandments of the Old Testament read regularly in early Christian worship,

48

enriched in their true significance by the interpretation given to them in the life and teachings of Jesus.

The two concluding verses of chapter one (1: 26-27) contrast vain religion with religion that is pure and undefiled before God. James presents this contrast, not by offering complicated definitions, but by giving vivid, concrete examples:

What sort of religion is vain (empty or useless)? That religion which does not teach its disciples to discipline their manner of speaking, the religion of those persons who continue to employ their tongues maliciously. James later observes that the perfect are able to bridle the whole body (3:2), but it was the need to bridle the tongue which seemed to be especially pressing in James' own day. He returns to the subject of the tongue in chapter three.

What sort of religion is pure in God's sight? James' answer is not exhaustive but is simple and direct: Visit orphans and widows in their affliction . . . keep [oneself] unstained from the world. Pure religion includes social ethics and personal ethics, outgoing love and inward steadfastness, serving in the world without becoming just like the world.

The orphan and widow had no defender and thus were often preyed upon or left to starve in the ancient world (Ezek. 22:7; Zech. 7:10; Mal. 3:5). The psalmist saw God himself therefore becoming a "father of the fatherless and protector (deliverer) of widows" (Ps. 68:5). The prophets (Zech. 7:6-10), the early church (Acts 6:1), and James believed that God's people must share his special concern for those most in need. To bring James 1:27 up to date, therefore, one ought to insert the names of those who, like the widows and orphans of old, are left without protectors and are therefore God's special concern in our day: society's outcasts and the forgotten poor, patients in the wards of overcrowded mental hospitals, defenseless victims of broken marriages, mistreated minorities, and others likely to be taken advantage of in market place or courthouse. Pure religion is to visit these needy ones as a willing servant of God's concern.

The words **religious** and **religion** used in verses 26 and 27 are rarely found in the New Testament. They are translations of Greek terms which emphasize the formal aspects of religion, the proper procedures for worship. James seems then to stand with the prophets of old (cf. Hos. 6:6) in declaring that, in God's judgment, true worship does not consist in words and gestures in the sanctuary. Discipleship is not measured according to the number of prayers said, Bible chapters read, or church meetings attended. *The heart of true worship is love at work where there is need, plus a faithfulness which will not be contaminated by the world's selfishness or desire for comfort.* Many helpful practices can enrich such worship, but nothing can replace it. **Religion that is pure and undefiled before God and the Father is this: to visit orphans and widows in their affliction, and to keep oneself unstained from the world** (James 1:27).

3

Commentary
on James
Chapters 2—5

In his opening chapter James has issued his call to grown-up discipleship. He has urged his readers to become mature disciples who have the power to endure and the will to put faith to work in the world. In the remainder of his book James enlarges upon specific areas in which Christians ought to grow up and practice the gospel. He uncovers the hypocrisy and immaturity he finds in some areas of church life and challenges the church to practice what it preaches. Both the painful truth of his accusations and the inescapable directness of his challenge seem especially intended for our day, our church, and ourselves.

Three special areas of concern with which James now deals at some length are *snobbery* (or partiality), *faith and works,* and the *use of the tongue.*

James' words directed against partiality or snobbery in the church are clear:

2:1-7 [1]My brethren, show no partiality as you hold the faith of our Lord Jesus Christ, the Lord of glory. [2]For if a man with gold rings and in fine clothing comes into your assembly,[1] and a poor man in shabby clothing also comes in, [3]and you pay attention to the one who wears fine clothing and say, "Have a seat here, please," while you say to the poor man, "Stand there," . . . [4]Have you not made distinctions among yourselves, and become judges with evil thoughts?

This passage is an excellent place to pause and compare English translations. That which the King James Version translates respect of persons and the Revised Standard Version calls partiality is more vividly translated by Phillips and *The New English Bible* as snobbery. "Don't ever attempt, my brothers, to combine snobbery with faith in our glorious Lord Jesus Christ!" (Phillips)[2]

---

[1] The Jewish background of James may be indicated here, for the word translated *"assembly"* is actually the Greek word for synagogue, used elsewhere in the New Testament only of Jewish places of worship.

[2] From *The New Testament in Modern English,* copyright J. B. Phillips 1958. Used by permission of The Macmillan Co.

Whatever one calls this sin of favoring the rich over the poor, its nature is the same: it is a lack of love. The rich, powerful, and prestigious can repay our favors with interest while the poor cannot. To reserve special attention for those who can further our own ambitions is to reveal the shallow and self-seeking nature of our relationships with others. "Love does not pursue selfish advantage" (I Cor. 13:5, Phillips).[1]

It is strange that the sin of snobbery or partiality should have become obvious so early in the life of the church. The church's Lord was born in a stable, apparently died penniless, and mingled less with the wealthy and powerful than with poverty-stricken peasants and society's outcasts. His concern was that "the poor have the good news preached to them" (Matt. 11:5). He is remembered as having said "blessed are you poor" (Luke 6:20), while warning that "you cannot serve God and Money" (Matt. 6:24, NEB)[1] He spoke the words, "It is easier for a camel to go through the eye of a needle than for a rich man to enter the kingdom of God" (Mark 10:25). His followers recognized that the earliest Christian community had "not many . . . wise according to worldly standards, not many . . . powerful, not many . . . of noble birth" (I Cor. 1:26). When asked for alms, Peter himself was forced to admit, "I have no silver and gold . . ." (Acts 3:6).

The church, however, not only soon gathered silver

---

[1] From *The New English Bible, New Testament.* © The Delegates of the Oxford University Press and the Syndics of the Cambridge University Press, 1961. Reprinted by permission.

and gold, but began to play favorites in order to encourage such gifts. It could no longer say, as had Peter to the lame beggar, "I have no silver and gold," but perhaps its growing interest in wealth also rendered it incapable of saying with Peter, "but I give you what I have; in the name of Jesus Christ of Nazareth, walk" (Acts 3:6).

Are the officials and members of the church in our own day guilty of the same sin James attacks: favoring the rich and powerful, neglecting the poor and shabby? Some years ago a sociologist found that he could successfully predict the denominational affiliation of a church building by knowing the wheelbase of the cars parked in front of it on Sunday morning. The coming of compact and foreign cars may make that impossible today, but is it not true that we in the churches increasingly separate ourselves according to class and wealth? Would a poor man [or woman] in shabby clothing feel welcome in our church? Would he be invited to come to church with us?

We must also ask whether our own standards within the church have been warped by the world's tendency to favor riches. What is our picture of the successful church? Is it the church that devotes its life to serving the needy who cannot repay, or is it the congregation that owns and administers property, that builds expensive structures, that attracts the wealthy families, and that wields power and prestige?

There may be another problem regarding the rich and the poor which especially belongs to our own day. Could it be that we have soothed our consciences by hiding the poor so that we might forget our ministry to them? It is said that the father of the future Gautama Buddha hid from the young boy's sight all elderly, poor, diseased, or disfigured persons so that his son, the young Prince Siddhartha, might believe that all the world was young, wealthy, healthy, and beautiful. Are we, like the father of Gautama, trying to raise a generation of children protected from ever seeing the elderly poor hidden away in overcrowded institutions, or the poverty and disfigurement of the city's hidden slums and the country shacks far back on dirt roads we never travel? If tenements do stand too close to the expressway, ironically enough they are blocked from view by billboards reminding us of cars, appliances, foods, and vacation spots that demand leisure and money. Do we on our Sunday drives seek out the homes of the favored rich and avoid the hidden neighborhoods of the poor and underprivileged? Perhaps the words of the condemned in Jesus' Parable of the Sheep and Goats will characterize our own children in a peculiar way: " 'Lord, when did we see thee hungry or thirsty or a stranger or naked or sick or in prison, and did not minister to thee?' " The answer given to those who ask this question in the parable is, "Truly, I say to you, as you did it not to one of the least of these, you did it not to me" (Matt. 25:44-45).

Perhaps in our day we have become so entangled in our possessions that we are no longer free to give ourselves in service to the needy. Like Marley, in Dickens' *Christmas Carol*, we have bound ourselves by the locks and chains of our acquisitions. Scrooge's words to Marley perhaps apply to us: "But you were always a good man of business, Jacob." And perhaps, like Marley's, our own awakening will come too late: "Business! Mankind was my business."

In his attack upon partiality, James asks: Has not God chosen those who are poor in the world to be rich in faith and heirs of the kingdom which he has promised to those who love him? (2:5)

Here we have the only reference to the kingdom in the Book of James, as well as the repetition of a phrase already encountered: those who love him (cf. 1:12). The coming of the kingdom is made certain by God's own promise, and the key to that kingdom is love.

That the poor in the world (by the world's standards) are especially chosen by God is often asserted in the Bible. God takes as his special concern those who have no other security. It is believed by some scholars that "the poor" was in fact a name by which the early Christian community described itself [1] (cf. Gal. 2:10).

James shows the foolishness of favoring rich over poor not only by pointing out God's special concern for the poor, but also by reminding the church how its members, often slaves and poor folk, have in fact suffered at the hands of the rich: Is it not the rich who oppress you . . . ? Is it not they who blaspheme that honorable name by which you are called? (2:6-7)

2:8-13   [8]If you really fulfill the royal law, according to the scripture, "You shall love your neigh-

---

[1] "'The beggars' became the honorable title for the messianic community." *The Interpreter's Bible*, Vol. X, p. 476.

bor as yourself," you do well. ⁹But if you show partiality, you commit sin, and are convicted by the law as transgressors. ¹⁰For whoever keeps the whole law but fails in one point has become guilty of all of it . . . .

Now James continues his attack upon this favoring of rich over poor by pointing out that it is against biblical law.

The royal law is: "'You shall love your neighbor as yourself.'" Perhaps James is reminding believers here of Jesus' great summary of the law of God's kingdom (see Matt. 22:37-40). Certainly he knows that the law he quotes is according to the Scripture recorded in the Book of Leviticus 19:17-18:

"You shall not hate your brother in your heart, but you shall reason with your neighbor, lest you bear sin because of him. You shall not take vengeance or bear any grudge against the sons of your own people, but you shall love your neighbor as yourself: I am the LORD."

Loving one's neighbor excludes favoritism of the select few who can further one's own ambitions.

James further clinches his case against partiality by arguing that this royal law of love cannot be ignored by a Christian even if he keeps every other law, for whoever keeps the whole law but fails in one point has become guilty of all of it. These words may seem particularly rigid and demanding, but they express an important truth which is often ignored. We cannot pick and choose among God's laws. God's store of commandments is not a supermarket where we pick only what is to our taste. There is a unity in

57

God's law. Ignoring or neglecting any part of God's law is a symptom of an immature or broken relationship between God and man or man and his neighbor and is a serious sin of omission, for the man who fails in one point has become guilty of all of it. Discipleship cannot be a matter of bookkeeping and balancing of commands obeyed against commands broken. Christianity at its heart requires an all-or-nothing commitment.

Finally, James reminds us that in judging persons according to their wealth, we are forgetting that we ourselves are to be judged . . . (2:12). If we expect mercy, we must practice mercy and remember that mercy triumphs over judgment (2:13; cf. Matt. 18: 23-35).

James has uncovered the painful fact that partiality exists within the church. He has challenged believers to banish this sin by aspiring to mature discipleship which expresses itself in true love of neighbor. James has shown us an unpleasant and deadly aspect of ourselves. He demands that as a church we put aside self-seeking favoritism and grow up in love.

Now James turns to a second major area of concern which uncovers the root of vain or empty religion: the separation of faith from works. Just as his discussion of partiality in favor of the rich echoed in part an earlier theme (cf. 1:9-11), so this lengthy discussion of faith and works (2:14-26) will echo a theme already sounded (1:22-27).

2:14-17 14What does it profit, my brethren, if a man says he has faith but has not works? Can his faith save him? ¹⁵If a brother or sister is ill-clad and in lack of daily food, ¹⁶and one of you says to them, "Go in peace, be warmed and filled," without giving them the things needed for the body, what does it profit? ¹⁷So faith by itself, if it has no works, is dead.

Here we arrive at the topic which many have singled out as James' major concern: the relationship of faith to works. Paul, the great Christian missionary, deals in depth with this same topic and places his emphasis upon faith: "a man is justified by faith apart from works of law" (Rom. 3:28). James appears to contradict Paul and seems to urge the opposite emphasis: Faith by itself, if it has no works, is dead (2:17). Whereas Paul (Romans 4) singles out Abraham as an example that one is "justified by faith," James claims that Abraham was justified by works and not by faith alone (2:21).

Does James intentionally urge an emphasis upon works which contradicts Paul's emphasis upon faith?

Some scholars suggest that James misunderstood Paul. Others claim that James is attacking followers of Paul who had distorted Paul's position. Note that II Peter 3:15-16 refers to Paul's views which "the ignorant and unstable twist to their own destruction . . . ."

It is possible, however, that James neither misinterprets Paul nor specifically attacks misguided followers of the Apostle. Rather it may be that he believed the moral crisis of his own day required a radically different perspective for viewing the relationship of **faith and works.**

Paul confronted many who insisted that they could earn God's favors by the strict observance of the laws of Judaism. He vigorously protested that none of us lives the kind of life that can make such claims for favor upon God. Christianity is built not upon our earning, but upon God's freely giving forgiveness and love. "Justification by faith" involves a turning to God in trust and perfect reliance upon his love alone. The Christian is not like the child who feels he must constantly work to earn his parents' love, but rather he is like the child who, trusting in his parents' freely given love, does his part in the family out of sheer happiness and gratitude.

James, however, is faced with quite a different situation. The issue is no longer whether one receives God's love by earning it or by receiving it in faith. Those to whom James speaks already claim to be Christians and claim to have faith, but in fact they insult the poor, gossip maliciously, and avoid their responsibilities toward those in need. James must begin at a different point from Paul. James does not speak of "works of law" which earn God's love, but rather points out that true **faith** cannot be **dead** or **barren.** A son should not need to earn his parents' love, but a son who has really entered into the family's love through responding trust and acceptance will be moved to take up tasks of love and cooperation within the family circle. If the son refuses to perform such tasks, it is a sign that something is basically wrong with his relationship to the family. It is here that James finds a key to the grave moral crisis of his day.

Focusing our attention on the text of James, we see that the author develops his argument on behalf of Christian works in three steps:

(1) Verses 14-17 (a parable)	To say you have faith, but not to act on it, is no more profitable than to say you are sorry for someone in need, but to make no effort to help him.
(2) Verses 18-19 (a dialogue)	To claim to have faith in God but to do no works actually is to do no more than merely profess that God exists, which even God's enemies (the demons) will do.
(3) Verses 20-26 (scriptural examples)	The stories of Abraham and Rahab demonstrate that true faith expresses itself in action. [Note the use of the words "active" and "completed" in verse 22.]

The first step compares one's claim to faith without works to one's seeing a brother or sister . . . ill-clad and in lack of daily food and saying to them, "Go in peace, be warmed and filled," without giving them the things needed . . . .

An old story tells of a boy who drops his basket of eggs on the way to market. Many people gather around to bemoan his loss and express their pity. Someone in the circle, rather than simply offering

pity, hands the boy a dime, saying "I care ten cents;
how much worth do the rest of you care?" There is a
wide chasm between the affirmations which are easily
made and cost us nothing, and the affirmations for
which we willingly spend ourselves and what is ours.
This is the chasm James finds between the claims to
faith of many in the church and real Christian faith
which spends itself in works of love. So faith by itself
if it has no works [and thus is not really the faith
of a disciple] is dead.

2:18-19   18But some one will say, "You have faith and
           I have works." . . . 19You believe that God is
           one; you do well. Even the demons believe—
           and shudder.

The second step in James' argument is an imaginary
dialogue. Some may claim that faith and works can be
an either-or for the Christian. James answers that any
so-called faith (or belief) in God that exists without
works is no more than a mere recognition of God's
existence which involves no personal commitment to
him, an acknowledgment which even the demons
make and yet remain God's enemies. In referring to
the belief that God is one, James may well be calling
to mind the famous Jewish *Shema,* the affirmation in
Deuteronomy 6:4 which comes closest to being Judaism's creed ("Hear O Israel: the LORD our God is
one LORD . . ."). The reference to the demons shud-
dering calls to mind the reported behavior of evil
spirits who recognize Jesus as "the Holy One of God"
(cf. Mark 1:24, 3:11).

2:20-26   ²⁰Do you want to be shown, you foolish fellow, that faith apart from works is barren? ²¹Was not Abraham our father justified by works . . . ? . . . ²⁵And in the same way was not also Rahab the harlot justified by works . . . ?

Abraham, regarded as the father of the Hebrew people, and Rahab, a Gentile prostitute who saved the lives of Hebrew spies in Canaan, are chosen as examples of persons whose faith was completed (or perfected) by works. But why should James choose such very different persons to reinforce his argument? Perhaps their very difference emphasizes James' point that all persons, from one extreme of society to the other, are to have faith that issues in works. Both Abraham and Rahab became popular figures in Hebrew tradition and thus serve as striking examples. Abraham appears also in Romans, chapter 4, both Abraham and Rahab appear in Hebrews, chapter 11, and Rahab is listed in the genealogy of Jesus in Matthew 1:5.

Note that for James, works are not emphasized to the exclusion of faith. On the contrary, he states that in the case of Abraham, faith was active along with his works and faith was completed by works. Likewise, when James states that Rahab . . . was justified by works he does not exclude faith. The "justification by faith" of which Paul spoke was the original act of trusting in God. James does not deny that faith is essential to this justification. But he emphasizes a subsequent requirement for the true disciple. Abraham revealed the liveliness and actuality of his faith by his obedient willingness to risk or to give up even the one thing he loved above all else, his male heir who would carry on the family name. Abraham's claim to faith was justified by his willingness to act on his faith. Likewise, Rahab's acceptance of two Hebrew spies as messengers of God expressed a faith upon which she was willing to act at the risk of her life.

It has often been pointed out that for Paul the word "faith" has a deeper sense which includes works whereas James has to add works to faith because of the pitiful shallowness and sterility of the faith professed by many in the church of his day. But this difference in the meaning of faith for Paul and James must not be overstressed. Paul too asserts the need for faith to perfect itself in works: "Faith working through love" (Gal. 5:6). He also recognizes a shallow faith which lacks an essential element: "If I have all faith, so as to remove mountains, but have not love I gain nothing" (I Cor. 13:2). The essential element missing from faith in James' day was works. Thus James announces the crucial fact: Faith apart from works is dead.

In James' day the moral crisis brought on by immature discipleship showed itself most vividly in a separation between believing and doing, faith and works. Is it not true that the church of our day faces a similar moral crisis, evident in a separation between what we profess and what we do? If this is true, then the Book of James has come of age once again and speaks directly to us the same urgent message originally delivered to our forefathers of almost two thousand years ago in this very same household of faith.

In 1963, J. Robert Moskin was commissioned by *Look* magazine to make a study of the present state of morality in the United States. From the resultant study based upon interviews with thinkers and leaders across the nation came the message: "Danger . . . . We are in the midst of a moral crisis . . . ." [1] Perhaps the spiraling crime rates have been enough to tell us this. Perhaps the frequent reports of bribed athletes, cheating by students, price rigging, discrimination, drug addiction, crime in the streets, fixed quiz shows, Hollywood love exploits, wife swapping, high school and college pregnancies, abortions, and unjustified congressional and labor union junkets and deals have awakened us to the seriousness of the extent of this crisis. Unfortunately the casual but too common excuse, "Well, *everybody's doing it*," is not infrequently made by persons who consider themselves good or who claim to be Christians. The cheating quiz contestant, husband, executive, or athlete is often from a good family and is not infrequently a church member in good standing. The crisis is within the church, not outside, yet those within the church claim to believe in a transformed way of life. Faith has again been separated from works.

A tax consultant not long ago told his pastor the reason for his cynical view of and disillusionment with the church: "I make out the tax returns and also

---

[1] "Morality U.S.A.," by J. Robert Moskin in *Look*, September 24, 1963. This article was reprinted by the Methodist Student Movement for conference studies. See "Recommended Materials," p. vi.

keep track of the church pledges for many of the members of this church. It's those who claim to be the most pious who swear on their tax returns that they give four times more to this church than I know they give."

Too often there is a sharp division between what church members say they believe and what they do.

Perhaps the gravest danger in this separation between faith and works within the church of our day is the fact that many of us have deluded ourselves into believing that we within the church measure up pretty well to God's standards. We often convince ourselves that our works do complete our faith.

The story is told of a church school teacher who taught her class a lesson on the Parable of the Pharisee and the Tax Collector. She pointed out how Jesus commended the tax collector's humble recognition of his sins but rejected the proud prayer of the Pharisee who thanked God that he was "not like other men, extortioners, unjust, adulterers, or even like this tax collector" (Luke 18:9-14). At the conclusion of the lesson, the teacher called upon all to bow their heads and prayed: "Lord, we thank thee that we are not like that Pharisee!"

Our church generation may not imitate the Pharisee's strict observance of every jot and tittle of the law, but we do seem to fall into the same trap of self-righteousness or pride as did both the Pharisee and the church school teacher. We thank God that we within the church do our share and more in this world. We point out the specks in the eyes of those outside our fellowship and miss the plank of hypocrisy lodged in our own eye. Do we, who claim to share in the New Testament faith, make any serious attempt to put the New Testament faith into practice?

The Sermon on the Mount begins by blessing the meek and those who mourn, and commanding us not to strike back when struck. Yet if Johnny acts meekly on the playground or refuses to strike back when struck, do we actually look upon him as "blessed" or do we say, "Listen, you have to learn to defend yourself and be a bit aggressive in this world of ours." If our teen-ager really began seriously mourning for the world's sins, would we count him "blessed" or would we consider taking him to a psychiatrist?

When we read Jesus' command, "Do not lay up for yourselves treasures on earth" (Matt. 6:19), does it really occur to us that our avid search for the better paying job, bigger bank account, and more comprehensive insurance plan separates the faith we claim in Jesus' view of life from our works? Do our works of personal love and concern really put us in the sandals of the Good Samaritan or in the habit of the priest and Levite who had pressing appointments and so avoided the one in need? Are we like the prodigal who returns on penitent knee from a life of selfish personal extravagances, or are we like the elder brother who wants all that is coming to him plus the exclusion of others who have been less calculating? When Jesus tells of the human impossibility of the rich entering heaven (Matt. 19:23-26), do we conveniently forget that, by the standards of Jesus' day, most Americans are rich? When we succumb to advertisements offering us luxuries, and advising us not to deny ourselves this or that, do we recall that we profess faith in a Lord who said, "If any man would come after me, let him *deny himself* and take up his cross daily and follow me"? (Luke 9:23)

The Bible does not advocate poverty for its own sake, nor should Christians condemn a rise in the standard of living when it is shared by all and not obtained at the expense of others. Affluence is not a crime in itself—it is the affluence which breeds self-centeredness that Jesus disapproves. The Samaritan was not condemned because he could afford to pay for the care of the man "who fell among thieves."

If we did not ourselves sell our integrity on a rigged quiz show, did we not enjoy watching those grown-ups play the rigged games with tens of thousands of dollars at stake? While we watched the games, perhaps we puzzled over why the younger generation had not learned the "value" of the dollar! The education editor of *The New York Times* recently warned that "a passion of possession" is being created among our youth. Have not we ourselves fostered that passion by evaluating success in life on the basis of income, property, or appliances? Do we judge people as successful, worthy, and valuable members of the community in terms of the outward signs of affluence? We may scoff at the singing "ads" which seek to persuade us that possession of a new model automobile will bring us an unheard-of sense of well-being and raise us above the petty cares of life, but do we not behave as if we have begun to believe such claims? And have we not instilled into the younger generation this gospel of property ownership? Jesus warned: "You cannot serve God and mammon" (property or money) (Matt. 6:24). *The New English Bible* translates this: "You cannot serve God and Money."

If our church in this generation is involved in such a critical separation between the faith we lay claim to and the works we practice, what are we to do?

We are already doing something. Serious study of the Bible leads us back to the source and reason for our existence as a Christian community. The biblical message judges our failures but also offers a cure for our ills. Christian ethics is in a sense "an extended footnote" on the "therefore" which unites the recital of what God has done for us to the exhortation of what we should do for him.[1] In order to respond in gratitude with works of love, we must first be confronted by God's acts of love recited in the biblical record which call forth that gratitude.

In our study groups and church services, we can also rediscover the meaning of the fellowship of the church. The study of I Peter which follows offers some guidance, but our study group itself, our family, and certainly our local congregation provide the perfect place to begin building one another up and practicing the faith we hope to put to work in our neighborhood and world.

Finally, we can take special note of the practical words of James, for he speaks to the church in just such a crisis. His next theme, in fact, is an excellent

---

[1] See James A. Pike, *Doing the Truth: A Summary of Christian Ethics* (Garden City: Doubleday & Co., 1955), p. 9.

place to begin if we are truly seeking to reconcile our faith to our works.

3:1-12 ¹Let not many of you become teachers, my brethren, for you know that we who teach shall be judged with greater strictness. ²For we all make many mistakes, and if any one makes no mistakes in what he says he is a perfect man, able to bridle the whole body also.

Having exposed the sins of partiality and of separating faith from works, James now turns his attention to the use of the tongue.

James' exhortation concerning the tongue is prefaced by a warning against many becoming teachers. This may call to mind Jesus' stern warnings to his disciples against their becoming like those Jewish teachers of the Law (rabbis or scribes) whose privileged position and pride often led them to act arrogantly, to impose burdens on others, and to use pious words which were mere pretense and a false front (Mark 12:38, 40; Matt. 23:2-12 ff.) Becoming a teacher has its special temptations and hence is not to be entered upon lightly. Those who teach, in fact, shall be judged with greater strictness (cf. Mark 12:40).

James refers to we who teach, thus giving us some clue to his own position in the church. It is possible that he himself may have been a Jewish teacher within the tradition of Jewish Wisdom Literature who heard the gospel concerning the Messiah and became a Christian teacher. The importance of teachers in the early days of the church may be indicated by the place Paul gives them in his list of gifted workers within the Christian community:

> God has appointed in the church first apostles, second prophets, *third teachers,* then workers of miracles, then healers, helpers, administrators, speakers in various kinds of tongues.
> I Corinthians 12:28; cf. Ephesians 4:11

As a teacher, James would have practiced that high calling, building upon the foundation of the gospel preached by evangelists such as Paul a solid structure of teaching, explaining the meaning of that gospel for all of life, and giving special emphasis to Christian morality or behavior as a thankful response to God's saving acts.

James' reference to teachers was probably inspired by his own involvement in teaching and the fact that the major tool of the teacher is the tongue. It is the tongue itself which now becomes his major concern.

If anyone makes no mistakes in what he says he is a perfect man, able to bridle the whole body also (3:2). Here James makes clear the connection between the coming discussion on the tongue and the main theme of his entire tract. In the quest to become a mature or perfect disciple (1:4), what one says plays a key role. If one can control even what he says, this is a good sign that he is able to control, to discipline the whole body also. This discussion on the tongue is also bound to the immediately preceding discussion of faith and works (2:14-26) and the earlier distinction between vain religion and religion that is pure and undefiled before God (1:26-27). Our *words* as well as our actions are works and should be consistent with our faith; otherwise religion is vain. Note, in fact, that immediately before his earlier definition of religion James introduced the subject he will now deal with at greater length: If any one thinks he is religious, and does not bridle his tongue but deceives his heart, this man's religion is vain (1:26).

James uses a number of similes and metaphors to describe the power of the tongue, most of which were popular, classical, or Jewish analogies: He compares the tongue to a bit in the mouth of a horse which guides the entire animal; to a small rudder which directs a great ship. So the tongue, though little, boasts of great things.

He states that the tongue is a fire. Unlike other creatures which can be tamed, the tongue is untameable and poisonous. Unlike a water-spring which yields only one sort of water, unlike a fruit tree which bears only one sort of fruit, the tongue utters both praises and curses. It should yield *one* sort of speech.

James' warnings concerning the tongue may once again identify him as a Christian Wisdom writer who felt a kinship with the authors of such Wisdom books as Proverbs and Ecclesiasticus.

Compare the above metaphors and similes employed by James, for example, with these passages of Proverbs:

> A worthless man plots evil,
> and his speech is like a scorching fire (16:27).
>
> . . . the mouth of the wicked pours out

evil things (15:28).

Death and life are in the power of the tongue,
and those who love it will eat its fruit (18:21).

The warnings of Ecclesiasticus (chapter 28) in the
Apocrypha are also worth comparing:

A hasty quarrel kindles fire,
and urgent strife sheds blood (v. 11).

The blow of a whip raises a welt,
but a blow of the tongue crushes the
bones (v. 17).

Many have fallen by the edge of the sword,
but not so many as have fallen because of
the tongue (v. 18).

Make balances and scales for your words,
and make a door and a bolt for your
mouth (v. 25).

Nor does James stand alone in the New Testament
in placing special emphasis upon our terrible responsibility for the use of the tongue and its words; Jesus
himself provides a foundation for such teaching:

For out of the abundance of the heart the
mouth speaks. The good man out of his good
treasure brings forth good, and the evil man out
of his evil treasure brings forth evil. I tell you,
on the day of judgment men will render account
for every careless word they utter; for by your
words you will be justified, and by your words
you will be condemned.

Matthew 12:34-37

Words, then, are works, and, because they spring
from the very source of our personality, they can be
a judgment for or against what we are in our inner
selves. Our words are an extension of our personality,

73

moving out like the ripples in a stream to touch all those about us for good or for ill.[1]

James indicates not only the powerful influence the tongue can have, but also its special susceptibility to the temptations and wickedness in the world: It is (or perhaps represents) an unrighteous world among our members (3:6). That the tongue also sets fire to the cycle of nature (3:6) may mean that it engenders destructive passions in the entire course or cycle of life, from birth to death (also see Phillips' translation of this passage).

What of our "words" and the use of our tongue in the church today? Is this a practical area for us as disciples to begin an examination and re-formation of our works?

Eugene Ionesco in his modern play *The Bald Soprano* [2] provides an illuminating critique of the debased state of words in our contemporary world. From the beginning of the play it becomes obvious that words have lost their connection with reality or truth. The actors expect to find no meaning in one another's words and hence use the tongue merely to play verbal games. Language becomes so irrelevant and debased that, shortly before the play closes, the actors have lost the power of human speech altogether and are simply barking and crowing.

Is Ionesco correct concerning the debasement of

---

[1] A study of the term "word" in *The Interpreter's Dictionary of the Bible* would be fruitful here, Vol. IV, pp. 868-72.

[2] Eugene Ionesco, *Four Plays: The Bald Soprano; The Lesson; The Chairs; Jack, or the Submission.* Trans. by Donald M. Allen (New York: Grove Press, 1958).

language, the separation of words from truth and reality in our day? What are the words we hear on radio and television or read in magazines and on billboards, day in and day out? Do they correspond to truth, to reality? Let us remember that the power of the tongue has now multiplied itself by these many new forms of communication. Is it true to reality that a certain brand of soap will give us "the wonderful glow of health," that smoking a certain cigarette indicates that one is a "thinking man," that a certain model auto will "make life worth living," that "a wonderful sense of security" depends upon a certain deodorant, or that a given after-shave lotion "will bring the women to you"? Though such claims may have little to do with reality, the "good news" they preach would not survive if we did not respond to it. This new gospel must therefore reveal something about our inner selves. Is it not strange that most of the tongue's activity, whether in advertising or polite conversation, deals with the gospel of *things?* We like to hear and talk about what we can own, what we must have, what treasures we have gathered or can gather for our personal comfort and security. Is it possible that, through such inaccurate or extravagant use of words, a forest is set ablaze, an entire culture is encouraged to count an illusory world of material values, comforts, and securities more desirable than the real world of God-given human dignity and person-to-person concern?

Can it also be that the feigned excitement of an announcer, gushing over dozens of products he has never used, has taught us to expect words to be divorced from reality? Have we trained our generation to use words to hide truth rather than to reveal it? Certainly words can be masks and deceptions which avoid rather than encourage honest personal relationships.

And what does the contemporary tongue's output of hate-literature, racial insults, and verbal character-assassinations have to say concerning the inner soul of our time? Have words simply become destructive weapons to further our selfish purposes and to give vent to our personal prejudices and frustrations, destroying those who stand in our path and are unable to defend themselves?

Unfortunately, in our day a visitor to this planet might not be able to distinguish professing Christians from others in the use of the tongue. Those who bless the Lord on Sunday can curse men Monday through Saturday. From the same mouth come blessing and cursing. My brethren, this ought not to be so (3:10).

Where can one begin in applying James' warnings concerning the tongue to daily life? Realization of the tremendous evil that the seemingly harmless tongue can work is a beginning, and acceptance of responsibility for our words as works with which to express our faith should follow. Are we guilty of murdering personalities, warping ideals, stunting growth and achievement, and of undermining the sense of responsibility in others with the weapon of the tongue? Have our words dwelt on self and property, setting up a distorted standard of values for a coming generation? If the spring or tree is good, its product is good. We must look to the source; we must grow up in discipleship. If our use of the tongue shows lack of wisdom, let us ask God, who gives to all men generously (1:5).

It is this theme of God-given wisdom as opposed to the earthly . . . wisdom to which James turns in the next passage.

3:13-18   ¹³Who is wise and understanding among you? By his good life [or "conversation"] let him show his works in the meekness of wisdom. ¹⁴But if you have bitter jealousy and selfish ambition in your hearts, do not boast and be false to the truth. ¹⁵This wisdom is not such as comes down from above, but is earthly, unspiritual, devilish.

The subject of the tongue seems to lead James now to examine the source of our speech and of our general attitude or posture in life. The source is wisdom, whether that from above which James called upon believers to pray for in 1:5, or earthly and devilish wisdom which breeds jealousy and selfish ambition. The good life (or "conversation," KJV) is marked by the meekness of wisdom ("the modesty that comes from wisdom," NEB). Concerning meekness, compare Paul's appeal to the "meekness of Christ" (II Cor. 10:1) and the words of Jesus, " 'for I am gentle and lowly in heart' " (Matt. 11:29). The source of such a life is the wisdom from above which James describes as pure, peaceable, gentle, open to reason, full of mercy and good fruits, without uncertainty or insincerity. Here we have a good description of James' view of God's manner of acting and of the similar conduct he expects among men. The characteristics produced by the opposite source, earthly or devilish wisdom, may well indicate the specific difficulties James encountered in the church of his day: bitter jealousy, selfish ambition, and disorder. One might suppose that James is championing peace and meekness as virtues necessary to cure strife and divisions comparable to those Paul battled in the church at Corinth (cf. I Cor., chap. 1) or that John deplores in III John. Perhaps James has in mind "false teachers" who on numerous occasions brought division and strife to the early church.

The following passage views further the disorders produced by reliance on earthly wisdom.

4:1-4   ¹What causes wars, and what causes fightings among you? . . . ²You desire and do not have; so you kill. . . . You do not have, because you do not ask.

Those whose life source is the wisdom from above are characterized by meekness and bring peace. Those whose life source is earthly or devilish wisdom are characterized by jealousy and selfish ambition and bring disorder. These disorders are now described as persistent wars or sudden, explosive fightings.

What is the cause of these disturbances? James asks. Is it not your passions that are at war in your members? (4:1) ("Do they not spring from the aggressiveness of your bodily desires?" NEB) James' question may refer to the strife within the individual (cf. I Peter 2:11; Rom. 7:23) or strife among the members of the congregation. Both meanings seem to be implied in this passage as a whole. How much of our energy is spent fighting wars within ourselves? Warring passions and divided loyalties can literally undermine the emotional and spiritual stability of an individual, injuring the psyche and leaving no energy for the living of life itself. Likewise, the "body of Christ," the church, can be torn apart by warring passions and divided loyalties, leaving no energy for the true mission of the church in the world. Too often our discouragement concerning the fightings which occur within present-day congregations leads us to sigh for the "good old days" of harmony and fellowship in the early church. A reading of Paul's Corinthian letters or this present section of James should remind us that such "good old days" are a fiction. From the beginning the church was plagued with divisive passions and fightings. This does not mean that we are therefore to acquiesce in such strife, but it does mean that we cannot use the present-day faults of the church as an excuse for unproductiveness and lack of mission! The early church poured out its life in a world mission in spite of inner fightings and outward tribulations.

When James goes on to speak of desire actually leading a person to kill, he is probably warning his readers of the eventual outcome of uncontrolled desire rather than referring to actual cases of murder in the church (cf. NEB). Another possibility is that he does see murder taking place in the sense I John speaks of it: "Anyone who hates his brother is a murderer . . ." (3:15).

James now turns in this passage to the theme of prayer, to which he referred previously in his discussion of wisdom (1:5-8). You do not have, because you do not ask (4:2). Earlier he had advised those who lacked the wisdom of mature disciples to ask God who gives to all (1:3). Again he makes clear that by all he means all who ask in faith and not the double-minded, so now he adds that others do not receive because they ask wrongly, to spend it on [their] passions (4:3). When our words are addressed to God but our thoughts firmly anchored on the shore of our own selfish interest, we ask wrongly. The guilty king in Shakespeare's *Hamlet* attempts to pray but finds:

> My words fly up, my thoughts remain below:
> Words without thoughts never to heaven go.
> (III, iii, ll. 97-98)

James' attack upon those whose life source is earthly or devilish wisdom comes to a climax with the words: Unfaithful creatures! Do you not know that friendship with the world is enmity with God? Therefore whoever wishes to be a friend of the world makes himself an enemy of God (4:4).

The words translated unfaithful creatures actually means "adulteresses," and is so translated in the King James Version of the Bible. The prophet Hosea spoke of Israel's worship of other gods as "adultery" against her one proper husband. The New Testament speaks of the church as the wife [bride] of Christ (cf. Eph. 5:23-32; Rev. 22:17). Jesus accused his generation of being an "adulterous generation." James may have this general body of imagery in mind, accusing those who are supposedly wed to God with running after other lovers, with leaving God in order to court the affections of the world.

What is the meaning of James' assertion that friendship with the world is enmity with God?

John 3:16 tells us that "God so loved the world that he gave his only Son . . . ." If God loved his creation and creatures, then certainly his followers should do so. In this sense the church ought to be "worldly"; that is, it should involve itself in all of God's creation and concern itself with each of his creatures. When cross and candlesticks or pious language interfere with the mission to the world, the Christian must be willing to put them aside and put on coveralls to serve the world in the way that effectively embodies God's love for his creatures.

But James is not using the word "world" in the sense of the creation and creatures God loves; rather he means by world that way of life which is popular in the world at large—the values and perspective of the age which are in contradiction to God's values and purposes and so separate us from our Creator.[1] He is saying, in a sense, what Paul says in Romans 12:2: "Do not be conformed to this world but be transformed by the renewal of your mind," which Phillips translates, "Don't let the world around you squeeze you into its own mold."

------

[1] It may be helpful here to read the article on "World" in *The Interpreter's Dictionary of the Bible*, Vol. IV, pp. 873-78.

4:5-10 [7]Submit yourselves therefore to God. Resist the devil and he will flee from you. [8]Draw near to God and he will draw near to you. (4:7-8)

Those who claim that the Book of James is a collection of unconnected sayings come closer to being correct from this point on. Although there still remains some continuity as James turns to advise those he has been admonishing as to the way back to the source of heavenly wisdom, there is a disjointedness to his words of exhortation. James 4:5 quotes as scripture a passage which either belonged to some book now lost or was a free rendering of an Old Testament theme: "He yearns jealously over the spirit which he has made to dwell in us." [1] This quotation is appropriate in view of the previous epithet "adulteresses." God will not abide rivals for the affection and loyalty of his disciples. In this sense he is a "jealous" God. James continues in verse 6 with a paraphrase of Proverbs 3:34 which we will meet again in I Peter 5:5, "God opposes the proud, but gives grace to the humble."

What can we as proud humans of double mind do to obtain God's grace or wisdom? James answers, submit to God. Resist the devil, draw near to God, cleanse, purify, humble yourselves. This entire movement of repentance seems to center in attitudes which are no more popular today than they were in James'

---

[1] See Burton Scott Easton, "Exegesis," *The Interpreter's Bible*, Vol. XII, p. 56.

day: *humility* and *receptivity*. This is the same response to God's goodness called for in James 1:19-21.

4:11-12 ¹¹Do not speak evil against one another, brethren. . . . ¹²There is one lawgiver and judge, he who is able to save and to destroy. . . .

Again James returns to a sin of the tongue. The Greek verb translated here by speak evil is *katalalein* and means to "talk against someone" or to "talk someone down," generally behind the person's back. The noun from this same root can be translated "slander," or, as in the King James Version, "backbiting" (cf. II Cor. 12:20).

It is interesting that James employs the words brethren and brother three times in this passage. Might it not be that *our* words concerning one another would be more considerate and constructive if we remembered that we are all members of one family?

James speaks against judging one's brother, reminding us of Jesus' own words: " 'Judge not, that you be not judged . . .' " (Matt. 7:1). Certainly this does not mean that we are not to be discerning, but rather that we should not seek to "play God" or pass fixed and final judgments. This is the prerogative of God alone. James' charge that to judge or condemn one's brother is to speak evil against the law may be taken as a reiteration of James 2:8, previously interpreted (see pp. 56-58).

4:13-17 ¹³Come now, you who say, "Today or to-
morrow we will go into such and such a town
and spend a year there and trade and get
gain"; . . . ¹⁵Instead you ought to say, "If the
Lord wills, we shall live and we shall do this
or that."

An acquaintance of mine was expecting some rela-
tives to spend a week's vacation at his home. He told
me that a portion of their letter giving their plans
read: "We will arrive at your home on Monday, God
willing. We will certainly arrive by Tuesday in any
event." Unintentionally, they may have used words
which are a parable of our times. Out of respect for our
tradition of piety we may allow God to tamper with
our plans to the extent of one day more or less, but we
will not tolerate his interfering any more seriously
than that. This is a far cry from the psalmist's words,
"Thou art my God. My times are in thy hand" (Ps.
31:14-15).

Certainly James' exhortation need not be taken in
a painfully literal fashion. We need not tag the words
if the Lord wills to our every sentence. We should,
however, cultivate that attitude of mind which dis-
cerns and invites "God's hand in all things, and all
things in his hand."

5:1-6 ¹Come now, you rich, weep and howl for the
miseries that are coming upon you.

Here James launches a somewhat unrelated tirade
against the rich, though there may be some connec-

84

tion between this verse and the phrase in verse 4:13: "trade and get gain." Compare our earlier comments concerning James' views on the rich in 1:9-11 and 2:1-7 (see pp. 38-39, 52-56).

James associates garments with riches (5:2), for an accumulation of expensive garments could (and still can) be a chief form of wealth in the Near East. James' warning to the rich that the rust of their gold and silver . . . will be evidence against you (5:3) may mean that one's wealth should have been put to service in life. Ecclesiasticus advises:

> Lose your silver for the sake of a brother or a friend,
> And do not let it rust under a stone and be lost.
> Ecclesiasticus 29:10

The law that the wages of the laborers should not be kept back by the rich is clearly stated in Leviticus 19:13 and Deuteronomy 24:14-15. In days when the poor laborer lived from hand to mouth, each day's wages were necessary for the family's daily bread.

It is possible that James had two purposes in mind in including a tirade against the rich at this point. First, he wished once again to warn the immature Christians of his day of the terrible temptations and consequences of attachment to material things. The very rich who easily fall into false security and abuse of power serve as a negative example for the less prosperous who are also tempted to devote life itself chiefly to the pursuit of perishable gold and garments.

Second, the impending judgment upon those who lived on the earth in luxury and in pleasure may set

85

the scene somewhat for the following exhortation to
the brethren that they await this coming time of
judgment with patience and steadfastness, knowing
that God in his own time will set right all the inequi-
ties and injustices of the world.

5:7-11   7Be patient, therefore, brethren, until the coming of the Lord . . . .

The early Christians believed themselves to be living in the critical time between these two key events
in world history:
  (1) God's humble and pain-filled visit to earth in
      the person of a helpless child, inaugurating the
      kingdom of love;
  (2) the imminent coming of Christ in glory to com-
      plete the establishment of that kingdom of
      love.
James calls Christians to patience and steadfastness
in view of this impending coming or *parousia* of
Christ in glory. He feels certain the coming is near,
though he makes no attempt to predict the date:
The judge is standing at the doors (cf. Rev. 3:20).
When Christ did not come in glory as soon as they
expected, Christians were perturbed; II Peter 3:8-10,
for example, attempts to explain the delay. Though
self-appointed prophets in our own day are constantly
claiming to know the exact timetable of the *parousia*
of Christ, James advises patience, which seems wise
in view of the words attributed to Jesus in Matthew,
"But of that day and hour no one knows . . ." (Matt.
24:36).

Samuel Beckett has written a tragi-comedy entitled *Waiting for Godot,* no doubt expecting that the reader will realize that the deletion of two letters will leave the title, *Waiting for God.* The play consists mainly of two actors on an almost bare stage, conversing and shuffling about rather aimlessly. The only reason they remain on stage at all seems to be a rather vague belief that "Godot" has promised to come, and so they wait. Exactly who "Godot" is, what he will do when he arrives, or why they should wait for him are questions for which they have no answer.

Much of our earthly existence may seem to be a succession of periods during which we are waiting on the stage of life for something new to happen. We wait to grow up, to own an automobile, to finish high school, to finish college, to marry, to raise a family, to retire (all of which are laudable ends in themselves). Finally we await death, possibly with some vague, undefined expectation of something more to come after death. Does our waiting have much more content than that of Beckett's characters? Not unless, like James, we as Christians understand our life here on earth to be a time of testing, a time of maturing as disciples, and of working out one's faith in the world. Christians, says James, should live in steadfast faith until the final consummation of God's purpose in the world, expectantly awaiting Christ's coming in some manner to complete his kingdom, a coming in accordance with his compassionate and merciful purpose evidenced in the manger, the cross, and the Spirit-led community.

5:12   ¹²But above all, my brethren, do not swear, either by heaven or by earth or with any other oath. . . .

Affirming the truth of one's words by swearing a special oath was apparently as popular a practice among the Jews as it later became among the Moslems (cf. Matt. 23:16-22). In the Near East it was customary to doubt the veracity of a person's words until he finally swore by the heavens and earth, or in the name of Allah, that he spoke the truth (cf. Matt. 26: 72).

Perhaps James is recalling here the words of Jesus: " 'Do not swear at all . . . . Let what you say be simply "Yes" or "No" . . .' " (Matt. 5:34-37; cf. Ecclesiasticus 23:9-11). The Christian should need no special oath to authenticate the truth of what he says or to distinguish special statements of truth from his everyday speech. Because the word of truth (1:18) has been the source of his life and has brought him into being, his "Yes" and "No" should always be spoken in honesty. Paul requires simple honesty from Christians on the grounds that they are all "members one of another" (Eph. 4:25).

5:13-18   ¹³Is any one among you suffering? Let him pray. Is any cheerful? Let him sing praise. ¹⁴Is any among you sick? Let him call for the elders of the church, and let them pray over him, anointing him with oil in the name of the Lord. . . . ¹⁶The prayer of a righteous man has great power in its effects.

As James' book of Christian Wisdom and moral exhortation draws toward its close, several final words of advice are strung together like beads on a string. Together they present a vivid summary of life as it should be for the disciples in the household of faith: Pray, sing praise, call for elders, confess your sins to one another. Among those who are disciples the suffering do not wallow in self pity but pray, the cheerful do not congratulate themselves but sing praise to God, the sick do not despair but call for the elders and find concern and prayer offered by the community on their behalf. Disciples can find forgiveness through the prayers of those to whom they confess their sins, for all are bound together in the acknowledgment that human life in the Christian community is made possible only through God's forgiveness which each can announce to his neighbor.

The reference to the elders who pray over and anoint the sick with oil is of special interest (cf. Mark 6:13). Apparently the Christian communities known to James were organized under the rule of elders (presbyters), in the manner of Jewish synagogues. Prayer and forgiveness seem to be the chief elements in this healing procedure, with the qualifying words "if the Lord wills" understood (cf. James 4:15). That the sick should be anointed with oil is not unusual. The famous Greek physician Galen spoke of oil as "best of medicines," and the Good Samaritan poured oil on the wounds of the one who fell among robbers (Luke 10:34). The Greek Orthodox Church takes this healing service described in James literally and regards *euchelaion*, as it is called, as a sacrament. The

Roman Catholic Church has come to emphasize the relation of this anointing service (or "unction") to forgiveness rather than to physical healing. "Unction" in Roman Catholicism has in fact developed into "extreme unction," a final supplement to the regular absolution, given after confession to prepare the believer for death. In our own day some Protestant groups are reviving interest in healing services which may include prayer and the anointing of the sick with oil by the elders of the church.[1]

5:19-20   [19]My brethren, if any one among you wanders from the truth and some one brings him back, [20]let him know that whoever brings back a sinner from the error of his way will save his soul from death and will cover a multitude of sins.

James, like the wisdom book of Proverbs, ends quite suddenly and unexpectedly. This final exhortation seems to be based on the preceding references to the responsibilities of disciples for the welfare of one another. James shows a special concern for those who wander from the true path of growing discipleship, for this was the chief problem and cause of the crisis in the church of his day. Every member, every one of us, James says, is responsible for bringing back those who have wandered from the pathway leading to mature discipleship. The Christian community is

---

[1] The Episcopal Church of the Heavenly Rest on Fifth Avenue in New York City and St. Stephen's Episcopal Church in Philadelphia are well known for their weekly services of healing in which the seeker is anointed with oil on the forehead by the minister.

knit together as a single body, and the welfare of each member should be a life-and-death concern to every other member. It is together that we are to mature as disciples. Whether the soul that is saved or the sins that are covered (cf. I Peter 4:8) are those of the wanderer or the one who brings him back is not clear in the text.[1] In either case, however, it is evident that the heart of James' closing exhortation is an affirmation that Christians are bound together in a community of concern.

---

[1] See "Exegesis," *The Interpreter's Bible*, Vol. XII, p. 73.

4

Commentary
on I Peter

Chapter 1

While the Book of James has sometimes been ignored or disparaged, I Peter, which immediately follows it in that group of books known as the Catholic Epistles or General Letters, has received almost universal praise. A wide variety of writers have referred to I Peter as "one of the most beautiful letters of the New Testament," "one of the finest and clearest examples of Christian teaching," "warm with the glow of a personal religion," "a moving piece of persecution literature," the work of one who was "as much a poet as a theologian," "a letter which has never lost its winsome appeal to the human heart." In view of such high praise from many sources, it is likely that the reading of I Peter will offer a moving and meaningful confrontation for the present day Christian who is willing to approach it thoughtfully and sensitively.

THE FIRST LETTER OF PETER

As is the case with James, the title appearing over this letter is a later addition. Originally the first few verses of I Peter gave the reader all the information necessary to identify the writing.

Unlike James, I Peter has both the salutation and the closing of a genuine letter. I Peter was probably an encyclical letter intended for circulation among the Christians in various parts of Asia Minor. Some scholars have noted, however, that I Peter 1:3 through 4:11 seems to form a self-contained unit concluding with its own doxology. They emphasize also that whereas the remaining section of the book, 4:12 to the conclusion, breathes the atmosphere of the fiery ordeal of contemporary persecution, 1:3 through 4:11 speaks of trials in a more general manner. For this reason some believe that I Peter 1:3 through 4:11 is a separate baptismal sermon directed to a group of new converts, a sermon considered worth preserving and sharing and therefore included within the text of the letter.[1] If this theory is correct, I Peter might be outlined thus:

| Salutation | (1:1-2) |
| A baptismal sermon | (1:3 through 4:11) |

[1] See, for example, F. W. Beare, *The First Epistle of Peter* (Oxford: Basil Blackwell, 1961), especially pp. 6-8, and F. L. Cross, *I Peter: A Paschal Liturgy* (London: A. R. Mowbray & Co. Ltd., 1954).

The letter proper—encouraging
   persecuted Christians   (4:12 through 5:11)
Closing greetings   (5:12-14)

There are other scholars who do not accept this theory since they do not recognize 1:3 through 4:11 as a separate baptismal sermon. They might therefore outline I Peter more simply:[1]

Salutation   (1:1-2)
Exhortations on the gospel
   and Christian life in trying times (1:3 through 5:11)
Closing greetings   (5:12-14)

After you have read the book, perhaps you will be able to decide for yourselves whether or not I Peter includes a separate baptismal sermon. In any case it is quite likely that the author was a Christian preacher who had issued the call to new converts to repent and be baptized so often that his use of the words obedience, newness of life, and salvation had become second nature to him and would thus be echoed and reechoed throughout his letter.

Such themes as Christian holiness, hope, steadfastness in adversity, new birth, following in Christ's steps, the expectation of Christ's glorious return, and the fulfillment of Old Testament promises are all woven together in the rich tapestry of I Peter's call to Christian living. The tapestry itself gains meaning as one perceives its two dominating motifs:

1. God's act (the gospel);
2. Man's response (the Christian life).

---

[1] See also Archibald M. Hunter, "I Peter: Introduction," *The Interpreter's Bible*, Vol. XII, p 85.

It is God's act of mercy which moves man to respond in a new life of joyful obedience. All the many themes of I Peter combine to form this pattern which weaves together inextricably God's act and man's response. These two motifs are again combined in a statement of the central purpose of I Peter at the conclusion of the letter: "I have written briefly to you, exhorting and declaring that this is the true grace of God; stand fast in it" (5:12).

It is because of God's act of mercy that the Christian finds strength and hope, and hence can remain steadfast even when rejected and dealt with maliciously by the society in which he lives.

1:1 Peter, . . . apostle of Jesus Christ, . . .

Once again we find the three-part salutation common in Greek letters of the first century (cf. James 1:1): (1) the writer's name, (2) the listing of those to whom it is addressed, and (3) a word of "greeting." In I Peter each of these three elements is given distinctive Christian content.

The first part of this salutation names Peter, an apostle, as the author of the letter. Was it actually Simon Peter, one of the twelve disciples chosen by Jesus, who wrote I Peter? Although scholars do generally agree that I Peter communicates the faith and concerns of early Christianity, they differ in their opinions concerning the identity of the author.

F. W. Beare and others who do not believe Simon Peter wrote I Peter point to a number of early Christian books written by unknown authors in Peter's

95

name.[1] Writing in the name of some famous personage was considered no more dishonest in the ancient world than is the present-day practice of employing ghost writers to prepare political speeches.

Those who question Simon Peter's authorship point out that:

1. I Peter is in excellent Greek, yet Simon Peter's native language was Aramaic and he could be described as an "unlearned and ignorant" fisherman (Acts 4:13, KJV).

2. I Peter seems to echo many of the thoughts of the Apostle Paul. Would Simon Peter, who showed an outstandingly independent spirit in all his dealings with Jesus, lean so heavily upon Paul?

3. I Peter says little about the earthly life and teachings of Jesus. Would not Simon Peter, once the close companion of Jesus, have included many narratives and sayings of the Master?

4. I Peter seems to have been written at a time when it was considered a crime to be a Christian. But this probably did not come about until the reign of Trajan (A.D. 98-117), long after Simon Peter's death.[2]

On the other hand, a number of scholars believe that I Peter carries the authority and message of Simon Peter himself. Here, in brief, is how they generally answer the above objections:

1. True, Simon Peter could not have written such

---

[1] See, for example, the books discussed in the articles "Peter, Apocalypse of," "Peter, Gospel of," and "Peter, Preaching of," in *The Interpreter's Dictionary of the Bible*, Vol. III, p. 756, pp. 766-67.

[2] See *The Interpreter's Bible*, Vol. XII, p. 79 (d).

excellent Greek, but Peter readily admits that someone who could write excellent Greek has aided him: By Silvanus, a faithful brother as I regard him, I have written . . . (5:12).

2. Silvanus is no doubt another name for Silas, a "prophet" who was one of the "leading men among the brethren" (Acts 15:22, 32) in the early church. Silvanus accompanied Paul on his "second missionary journey" (Acts 15:40 ff.) and is listed as a co-author of the two epistles to the Thessalonians (I Thess. 1:1; II Thess. 1:1). No doubt Simon Peter could allow such an accomplished missionary as Silvanus considerable freedom in framing a message to Christians in Asia Minor, and no doubt Silvanus' association with the Apostle Paul would lead to the inclusion of Pauline thought in such a document.

3. Whether I Peter really lacks personal references to Jesus' life and words is open to dispute. Some scholars find many echoes of Jesus' teachings and reflections of his personal thought and feeling in I Peter. If these echoes are less obvious than one would expect in a letter written by a companion of Jesus, one must remember that the great events of the crucifixion, the resurrection, and the continuing guidance of the risen Christ overshadowed the biographical details of his earthly ministry for early Christians.

4. The belief that certain references in I Peter which indicate that it was written at a time when it was a legal crime to be a Christian and that the persecution of the Christians did not occur until the reign of Trajan and hence long after Simon Peter's death, seems based on far too rigid an interpretation

of I Peter and far too limited a view of the history of Christian persecution. References in I Peter to suffering "for the name of Christ" may refer to malicious acts of suspicious pagan neighbors, or mob violence later encouraged by Nero's accusation that the Christians had burned Rome (A.D. 64), rather than to legal action against them. That personal violence against adherents of an unpopular cause can be countenanced by local authorities and encouraged more by unspoken attitudes of officials than by legal pronouncements becomes evident as one studies the confusing history of racial violence in our own day.

Presuming that the faithful brother Silvanus was a trusted aid to Simon Peter in the framing of this letter, evidence would seem to favor the long-standing church tradition [1] which views Simon Peter, one of the Twelve, as author of I Peter.[2] The letter may well have been written in the early sixties from Rome (cf. comments on 5:12-14).

In his salutation, Peter describes himself simply as an apostle of Jesus Christ. The word apostle comes from the Greek verb *apostello* which means "to send forth"; it is a title describing a person commissioned and sent out as a messenger or ambassador by some ruler or power. An apostle bears the authority and the message of the one who sends him, much as an Ameri-

---

[1] The fourth-century church historian Eusebius could refer to I Peter as "genuine and acknowledged by the elders of former days," though he writes of II Peter as "not stamped in the same way as canonical works."

[2] See *The Interpreter's Bible*, Vol. XII, p. 78.

can ambassador represents and speaks for America in other countries. So eleven of the Twelve whom Jesus originally chose, commissioned, and sent out (Matt. 10:2), and Matthias, "enrolled with the eleven" (Acts 1:26) in place of Judas Iscariot after the Resurrection, and Paul who received a belated commission (Gal. 1:1), have a special right to the title apostle. In a wider sense it seems that it can also be applied to others besides the Twelve and Paul (cf. I Cor. 9:5 f.; Rom. 16:7).

Is it possible to describe oneself without centering attention on one's own person? This is exactly what Peter has done. The word apostle calls attention, not to Peter himself, but to Jesus Christ who has commissioned him and sent him with a message. Our own self-descriptions no doubt similarly reveal the center of our life-interest, indicating whether it resides in a personal self-centeredness or whether our life has been caught up by some cause or message beyond self which sends us out into the world as servants or apostles.

According to the Gospels, the name "Peter" was not the original name of this member of the Twelve. Simon Bar-Jona is given the name Cephas (Aramaic) or Peter (Greek) meaning "rock" or "stone." Jesus apparently encouraged and challenged Simon to earn the new name "Rock," for although Peter would sleep in Gethsemane and later deny his Lord, he was commissioned to "strengthen the brethren" (Luke 22: 31 ff.). The aim of this very letter, I Peter, is just this: "to strengthen the brethren."

1:1-2 ¹To the exiles of the dispersion in Pontus, Galatia, Cappadocia, Asia, and Bithynia, ²chosen and destined by God the Father and sanctified by the Spirit for obedience to Jesus Christ and for sprinkling with his blood:

Part two of the salutation names those to whom **Peter** (through Silvanus) addresses the letter: **To the exiles of the dispersion.**

We have already seen that James addressed the Christian church as "the twelve tribes in the dispersion," the New Israel scattered in the pagan world (James 1:1). Peter uses a similar form of address. Just as Jews scattered outside Palestine still looked back to Jerusalem as their home, so Christians—scattered among neighbors often suspicious and unfriendly—looked to a homeland shared by all of the "household of God," a homeland "kept for them in heaven" (cf. 1:4; Phil. 3:20). Christians are born citizens of a new land and must display the best manners of that new citizenship while they are traveling abroad on earth. Earthbound men will then note the exile's behavior and may be awakened to the fact that there is another land with another way of life (cf. 1:17; 2:11). Thus the Christian exile, in any age, has an awesome responsibility for his conduct while on earth.

A second-century essay entitled *The Epistle to Diognetus* describes Christians thus:

They live in their own countries but only as temporary residents. They have a share in responsibilities as citizens, and endure all things as foreigners. Every foreign land is their fatherland, and yet for them every fatherland is a foreign land. . . . They busy themselves upon earth, but their citizenship is in heaven.[1]

Is this then the secret or the key to the secret of the early church's mission? It understood itself as here on earth commissioned to work where there was need, yet clearly committed to a higher loyalty which would not conform to the popular mores and self-satisfactions of the world. Its members "busy themselves upon earth, but their citizenship is in heaven."

The word exiles might also be translated "sojourners" (cf. Gen. 23:4) or "pilgrims." Perhaps if Peter were writing today he would speak of Christians as "God's Peace Corps," on their best behavior away from their real homeland, commissioned to serve wherever there was need as representatives of the concern of their fatherland. It is easy to see how this early church "peace corps" captured men's imaginations in the first century A.D. when we consider the immediate and enthusiastic response to our recently established national Peace Corps. It is also evident that our present-day church has lacked to a large extent the spirit of enthusiasm and mission of the Peace Corps, since it was government initiative and not church leadership that inspired so many laymen to enlist in active service to the world in need.

The exiles or "pilgrim" Christians addressed by Peter were scattered across five sections of Asia Minor (present-day Turkey) which at that time made up

---

[1] *Epistle to Diognetus* 5:5. See also "Exposition," *The Interpreter's Bible*, Vol. XII, p. 89.

four Provinces of the Roman empire.[1] The order in which they are named in I Peter may indicate the circular route the bearer of the letter would take after starting perhaps at Sinope in Pontus.

This brief address to the exiles is packed with theological content: they are chosen and destined by God the Father and sanctified by the Spirit for obedience to Jesus Christ and for sprinkling with his blood.

Note that God the Father . . . the Spirit . . . and Jesus Christ are all mentioned in this brief passage (cf. II Thess. 2:13-14). Could the reference to the Trinity be meant to remind those addressed of the formula employed at their baptism: "In the name of the Father and of the Son and of the Holy Spirit" (Matt. 28:19)?

In the words chosen [or elect, KJV] and destined by God, Peter epitomizes the history of Israel, the "chosen people." He reminds the scattered Christian minority in Asia Minor that, though they may appear lost among the pagan masses, they are in fact the inheritors of all God's plans for his world.

They are sanctified or "made holy" by the Spirit. Here again the writer may be referring to their baptism, for at baptism believers are sanctified, born anew, or set apart as God's special people.

Holiness or sanctification is not, however, something one puts in a safe-deposit box as a proud possession. The exiles are sanctified for a purpose: for obedience to Jesus Christ. Holiness or sanctification is not

---

[1] For the history and characteristics of Asia Minor in biblical times, see the article "Asia Minor" in *The Interpreter's Dictionary of the Bible,* Vol. I. pp. 257-59.

a pious excuse for noninvolvement in the world. Because a Christian has been "set-apart," made "holy," or sanctified for God's service, he can become fully involved in our world in a positive and transforming way. The sanctified believer has been purged of vested interests in the world; the world cannot "pay him off" or buy his vote. He does not serve the world in order to gratify himself but out of obedience to Jesus Christ. Obedience is a key word in I Peter and we will return to it.

The exiles are also sanctified . . . for sprinkling with his blood. These words may seem strange to us, but they are important to the whole pattern of Peter's thought. Their meaning becomes clearer if we remember that the two parts of our Bible might more accurately be called the Old and New Covenants rather than the Old and New Testaments. The story of the sealing of the Old Covenant between God and man at Mount Sinai is told in Exodus:

Moses . . . took the book of the covenant, and read it in the hearing of the people; and they said, "All that the Lord has spoken we will do, and we will be obedient." And Moses took the blood and threw it upon the people and said, "Behold the blood of the covenant which the Lord has made with you . . . ."

Exodus 24:7-8

Moses took the blood of sacrificed oxen and sprinkled half on God's altar and half on the people to seal God's living agreement to be their Lord if they in return would be obedient. Blood was believed to contain the life-force of a creature; hence, this ceremony bound God to his people by the force of life itself. Peter and the early church saw Christians as the new "chosen people" of God bound to the Father by a new covenant. This New Covenant had also been sealed with the life-force of a blood sacrifice: "This cup is the new covenant in my blood" (I Cor. 11:25). God's own act in the life of Christ bound the New Israel to its God with bands of sacrificial love.

Throughout I Peter we find this deep sense of the applicability of the history of Israel to the church, the sense of God's preparation for his new people[the church] through the history of the old people [Israel]:

Old Testament
    Covenant at Sinai
    Inheritance of Promised Land
    Israel as God's Servant

I Peter
    Covenant through Christ
    New Inheritance (cf. 1:3-25)
    New Israel as God's Servant (cf. 2:1-10)

The exiles, then, are the new key to God's plan for his world, set apart and purged of vested interests by the Spirit, prepared for obedience and bound to God by his costly outreach toward men in Jesus Christ.

1:2 May grace and peace be multiplied to you.

As we have already seen in our study of James, the third and final part of the salutation of a letter was often simply the word *chairein* (greeting). Peter, however, employs another word taken from that same root, the word *charis* (grace). To grace he adds another greeting: *Irene* (peace). Grace is used in the New Testament for the unmerited love of God shown in Jesus Christ. Peace for the Hebrew meant much more than the mere absence of war. It meant health and harmony, the completion of God's work of salvation for all creation. Peter's word of greeting thus becomes a prayer that Christians might increasingly appropriate God's freely given love and come to know the harmony which begins in a new relationship between God and man and finally blossoms in the wholeness of God's reign in the cosmos.

1:3-5 ³Blessed be the God and Father of our Lord Jesus Christ! By his great mercy we have been born anew to a living hope through the resurrection of Jesus Christ from the dead, ⁴and to an inheritance which is imperishable, undefiled, and unfading, kept in heaven for you, ⁵who by God's power are guarded through faith for a salvation ready to be revealed in the last time.

The body of the letter, which may be the beginning of a baptismal sermon, introduces us at once to the richness of the tapestry of the Christian faith. The first of the two major motifs of I Peter, *God's act,* dominates, though the second, *man's response,* is already woven into its fabric by the reference to believers as born anew.

Blessed be ... God. It is not unusual for a letter to begin with a doxology or blessing directed to God.

Paul begins II Corinthians similarly, and Jewish worship regularly included a blessing of God (cf. Ps. 34, 134, 144). Jewish blessings of God often concentrated upon his work in creation and his redeeming act which saved Israel from Egypt. Peter again parallels the Old Covenant as he blesses God's new creation (we have been born anew) and new redemptive act (through the resurrection of Jesus Christ).

The distinctively Christian viewpoint is immediately evident for Peter blesses not the God of Israel, but "the God and Father of our Lord Jesus Christ." The Christian has come to know God through God's own act in Jesus Christ.

We have been born anew not by the merit of man, but by the mercy of God. Jesus himself spoke of the need for a new birth: "You must be born anew" (John 3:7). New birth is associated with baptism in Romans 6:1-5 where baptism is described as burial with Christ and rising with him that "we too might walk in newness of life." God's act of mercy works a radical change in man's existence, comparable to beginning life all over again.

Most of us have known someone whose outlook on life has been dramatically changed by a catastrophe or blessing and we have said, "Why, he is like a new person!" Peter envisioned such a radical change being worked in the believer. This sense of a completely new beginning must be part of what Jesus meant when he said, ". . . unless you turn and become like children, you will never enter the kingdom of heaven" (Matt. 18:3). Leaving the fishing nets, whose use we have mastered, and enrolling in Christ's kindergarten, to begin the new schooling in discipleship, is both a humbling and a refreshing experience.

Too often our age ignores the need for such drastic reorientation. Though we sense sickness in the old way of life, we attempt to apply band-aids to heal a broken spirit and a failing heart, and we are therefore continually frustrated and disappointed. "You must be born anew."

It is through God's act in the resurrection of Jesus Christ, through God's willingness to become involved, to suffer, and yet to have the final word over sin and death, that we have been born anew. Dying to our old manner of life, we become related to Christ and are raised with him to a new quality of living. This new life is described by Peter as being born into:

1) A living hope
2) An inheritance
3) A salvation

All three of these gifts of the new life look toward the future, for even salvation is spoken of as ready to be revealed in the last time. Peter sees the Christian's life focused in anticipation on the future culmination of God's plans. The Christian knows the character of God's acts in the past and so can participate confidently in the present and look expectantly toward the future consummation of all things.

The Christian's living hope is in contrast to the weariness of the world's disappointment and frustration, the fading of all its dreams. Ephesians 2:12 speaks of the world apart from God as "having no hope," and Shakespeare's Macbeth paints a bleak picture of life without hope:

Life's but a walking shadow; a poor player,
That struts and frets his hour upon the stage,
And then is heard no more: it is a tale
Told by an idiot, full of sound and fury,
Signifying nothing.

Act V, Scene v, 11. 24-28

Earthbound hopes directed to the acquisition of a little more money, a little more time, a new job, a new hobby, a new neighborhood are subject to the world's natural process of decay and in the end may bring only disappointment and the death of hope itself.

Peter's description of the Christian's inheritance as imperishable, undefiled, and unfading is surely intended to point up the contrast between his "living hope" and the hopes which the world counts important but which perish, are defiled by evil, and fade with time. Christians, in contrast to men of the world, inherit citizenship in a new homeland beyond decay and death. They are "heirs of God, and fellow heirs with Christ" (Rom. 8:17).

By God's power believers are guarded through faith for a salvation . . . . Though Christians live in hope they are not to be unrealistic. This present pilgrimage, this work-colony of God on earth, is besieged by earth's dangers, deceptions, and cruelties. The Greek word for guarded is a military term. God "garrisons" his colony on earth. Christians are to be constantly on watch, armed (cf. 4:1) with the weapons God provides as described in Ephesians 6:13-17: "Therefore take the whole armor of God, . . . the shield of faith . . . the helmet of salvation, and the sword of the Spirit . . . ."

1:6-7   ⁶In this you rejoice, though now for a little while you may have to suffer various trials . . . .

"Sour godliness is the devil's religion." Because Christians are born anew to a living hope, an imperishable inheritance, and salvation, they ought to rejoice (1:6; 4:13) with exalted joy (1:8). The Christian knows of the unfolding plan which will dominate history, he has been assigned a vital task in the working out of that plan, and he is assured that the new age is about to dawn. Who is in a better position to rejoice and to love life (cf. 3:10)?

For a little while you may have to suffer various trials. Here the reference to trials does not speak of them as present or inevitable, though the phrase fiery ordeal of 4:12 ff. does seem pressing and immediate. As noted earlier, some would explain this difference by assigning 1:3 ff. to an incorporated sermon (see pp. 105-6) and 4:12 ff. to the letter proper written directly to readers faced by persecution. Another possibility is that, between the writing of this earlier part of the letter and the part dealing with the fiery ordeal in 4:12 ff., news of an outbreak of persecution in Asia Minor had reached Peter and Silvanus in Rome.

Concerning the significance of trials (*peirasmois*) in the Christian life, see the extended discussion of James 1:2-4 in Chapter II (pp. 30-34). Note that James also associates trials and testing with joy. If gold is tested and purified in refining furnaces, even more should faith, which exceeds gold in value, be subject to refining fires (cf. Prov. 17:3). Life's obstacle course, to change the metaphor, exercises and disciplines the Christian athlete; life's battles train the Christian soldier. Persecutions test his faith, and that faith, having been proved genuine, will earn for the Christian praise, glory, and honor at the revelation ("unveiling" or "appearance") of Jesus Christ. (Cf. NEB and Phillips.)

Are joy and the suffering of trials which appear together in this passage really compatible? At one time it was not uncommon for Christians to gather at the deathbed of one of their members to sing hymns of rejoicing. The trial of grief at parting and the joy of a loved one's completing life's pilgrimage and entering the mystery of God's presence were experienced together. In a poem by the Puritan poet Edward Taylor, the poet's grief at the death of his young children is mingled with his joy that he has been found worthy of raising such beautiful "flowers," which God has picked to decorate the heavens. The joy that can flourish in grief as well as in pleasure is the deeper joy which belongs in the list of "fruit of the Spirit" (cf. Gal. 5:22).

1:8-9 ⁸Without having seen him you love him; though you do not now see him you believe in him and rejoice with unutterable and exalted joy. ⁹As the outcome of your faith you obtain the salvation of your souls.

The Christian's joy is not simply in trials or in the expectation of future blessedness. Faith is the Christian's key which opens the door of the future and allows the light of that larger room to reveal a new dimension of present existence for the Christian. Through faith the Christian is already related to the invisible Christ in love. For the meaning of love (*agape*) in the early church one might examine the article on "Love" in *The Interpreter's Dictionary of the Bible*, trace the word in a concordance, or read the thirteenth chapter of I Corinthians. Compare with this present passage Jesus' words according to John (20: 29): "Blessed are those who have not seen and yet believe."

If Peter is the writer of this passage, the reference to those who have not seen Jesus may be contrasted to his own position as one who had been privileged to know and accompany the Galilean during his earthly ministry. Peter had also experienced "salvation," the result of that "faith" which relates the believer to his Lord in "love"—the endowment of the sum of God's gifts to man, a total transformation of life.

1:10-12   ¹⁰The prophets who prophesied of the grace that was to be yours searched and inquired about this salvation: ¹¹They inquired what person or time was indicated by the Spirit of Christ within them when predicting the suf-

III

ferings of Christ and the subsequent glory
. . . .

The ancient cathedral of Chartres in France has a window which pictures the four evangelists, each seated upon the shoulders of an Old Testament prophet. This close association of the gospel with the Hebrew prophets was a major presupposition of the preaching of the early church (cf. Acts 2:15-36) and is vividly expressed in this passage from I Peter. God's act in Christ was no accident or sudden whim of the Divine. Christianity is built upon the long history of God's dealing with his people Israel.

The unity of God's acting in the Old and New Covenants is made clear as Peter notes that the same Holy Spirit or Spirit of Christ spoke through the prophets and through those who preach the good news to you (the Christian evangelists). Likewise, the content of the message of Hebrew prophets and Christian evangelists is the same: the good news or the sufferings of Christ and the subsequent glory.

Christ's sufferings remain in the foreground in Peter's thinking and are referred to on several occasions in this letter. The reference to prophetic predictions of such sufferings probably points to the "suffering-servant songs" of Isaiah.

The key point at which the Christian finds himself in history is dramatically underscored in Peter's explanation that the Hebrew prophets themselves realized that their predictions would be fulfilled, not in their own time, but in the future and that they thus served not themselves but later generations (cf. I

Cor. 9:10). Peter even pictures the angels as eager
to discover the way in which God will work out his
plan for the believers.

1:13-17   [13]Therefore gird up your minds, be sober,
           set your hope fully upon the grace that is
           coming to you at the revelation of Jesus
           Christ. [14]As obedient children, do not be
           conformed to the passions of your former
           ignorance, [15]but as he who called you is holy,
           be holy yourselves in all your conduct . . . .

Having focused thus far largely upon *God's act,*
Peter now concentrates upon the second of the two
major motifs in his rich tapestry of faith: *man's response.* The remainder of I Peter, chapter 1, is a call
to the believer to make such a response.

Live obedient and holy lives because:

1. He who called you is holy (13-17);
2. You were ransomed with the precious blood of
   Christ (18-21);
3. You have been born anew (22-25).

In our study of James we discussed the vital
significance of the word therefore in Christian ethics.
God has worked wondrous things for man; therefore
the believer responds wholeheartedly in a new life
which is obedient and holy.

Therefore gird up your minds. Before beginning
vigorous activity, persons who habitually wore long
robes would reach down, pull up the hems of their
garments, and tuck them into their belts—they "girded
their loins." The Christian is to prepare the center of

his powers of discernment for vigorous activity. The church calls upon both body and mind to "come dressed for work."

Some seem to believe that one ought to leave one's mind in the vestibule when entering a church. Unfortunately, we often encourage such an idea. Though we may refuse shoddy products out in the world, too often, once we enter a church, we expect and accept superficial and sentimental sermonizing, we employ pious generalizations in answer to hard questions discussed in the church school, we are content with fourth-rate gospel jingles set to waltz time, or we cherish fifth-rate religious art. Sermons, teaching, music, and art within the church should be second to none, yet too often they are inferior because we fail to apply to them the test of the "girded mind."

Bible study in the church frequently suffers the same fate. We joke about the fifth-grade boy who complains that he just can't learn names and dates for history class but happily rattles off the name, date, and batting average of every major league baseball player. Are we not often guilty of the same self-deception? Studies in the Bible are "too hard," or "demand knowledge of special vocabulary." Yet we learn the special vocabulary of each year's new fashions and hairdos or find ourselves using the technical terms of the space age, or atomic physics, or the jargon of Westerns and monster shows on TV. If we are serious about our own faith should we not individually heed this call to Gird up [our] minds so that we may do our part in mentally equipping the household of faith?

The Christian is also called to be sober—to be in complete control of all his senses—and to set hope fully upon the grace that is coming—to work in confidence that God's final word in history will soon be spoken. Peter's readers must not be conformed to the passions of [their] former ignorance (cf. Rom. 12:2). Advice of this kind was often given to former pagans, and may indicate that the readers in Asia Minor addressed in this letter were largely new converts.

"It is written, 'You shall be holy, for I am holy.'" Here, in words from Leviticus 11:44-45, is the heart of the first of three reasons given for the converts' new way of life. Believers are to share the character which sets their God apart from all else. One might compare Jesus' words: "You, therefore, must be perfect, as your heavenly Father is perfect" (Matt. 5: 48). The word holy comes from the same root as the word sanctified which we discussed earlier (see our comments on I Pet. 1:2). Another word from this same root is "saint." Because believers have been sanctified, called to be holy, or "set apart" for God's own purposes, they can be called "saints" (Rom. 1:7; Eph. 1:1). Believers look to God as their standard and example; they need not rely upon the praise of men or follow the fashion of the world, "the way things have always been done" on earth. Christians have a unique freedom. They have a "polestar" beyond earth's changing fancies by which to set their course.

When in verse 17 Peter refers to those who invoke as Father him who judges each one, he may well be thinking of congregational prayer during worship services, perhaps the praying of the Lord's Prayer in which God is invoked as Father. Again he reminds his readers that their stay on earth is a time of exile, and that, as visitors upon earth, they should watch seriously the example their behavior sets earth's citizens. The same God who is Father also judges; they must give a strict accounting of their conduct before him.

1:18-21 ¹⁸You know that you were ransomed from the futile ways inherited from your fathers, not with perishable things such as silver and gold, ¹⁹but with the precious blood of Christ, like that of a lamb without blemish or spot . . . .

The second reason given the Christian for taking this new life of holiness and obedience seriously is the tremendous price paid to make the new life possible. Here the language both of the slave market and of Hebrew sacrifice is employed. Just as a slave in the ancient world could be purchased from his master with silver or gold, so believers have been ransomed from their bondage to futile allegiances. Christians have been "bought with a price" (I Cor. 6:20). The purchase made by Christ, however, was of a different order, for he did not pay with perishable silver and gold but rather with his own life's blood.

As he wrote these words, it is possible that Peter had in mind the Passover lamb whose blood once marked the homes of the Israelites in Egypt and saved them from death (Exod. 12), or the blood-sacrifices of the Temple (cf. Heb. 9:12), or Isaiah's description of the "suffering servant" led "like a lamb to the slaughter" (Isa. 53:7).

Christ, God's outreach to mankind in love, was conceived even before the foundation of the world. God has been at work, Peter affirms, planning through the ages this saving event which shall take place through Christ at the end of the times for your sake. Apparently Peter envisions the church as continuing to exist to the end of the times, the last days (cf. Heb. 1:2; Acts 2:17 ff.), waiting in confidence for the consummation of all things.

1:22-25   [22]Having purified your souls by your obedience to the truth for a sincere love of the brethren, love one another earnestly from the heart. [23]You have been born anew, not of perishable seed but of imperishable, through the living and abiding word of God; . . . . [25]That word is the good news which was preached to you.

The third and final reason given here for the leading of a holy and obedient life is the fact that through the word of God the believer has actually been born anew [1] (see pp. 105-7; cf. our comments on 1:3).

---

[1] F. L. Cross, who believes I Peter to contain an early Christian Easter baptismal service, suggests that the actual baptism of converts occurs between 1:21 and 1:22. In 1.22, therefore, the converts can be spoken of as "purified" and "born anew." See *I Peter: A Paschal Liturgy* (London: A. R. Mowbray & Co. Ltd., 1954), pp. 38-39.

Note that Peter associates imperishable seed, word of God, and the good news (gospel). We might compare this passage with the interpretation of Jesus' Parable of the Sower: "the sower sows the word . . . those that were sown upon the good soil are the ones who hear the word and accept it and bear fruit . . ." (Mark 4:14 ff.).

It is of special interest that the only occurrence of the word truth in I Peter is in this passage. What is truth for Peter? An idea or philosophical proposition to be meditated upon or accepted? No, for Peter, truth is something more; a concept, a plan of life, to which one can be obedient. Christians *do* or follow the truth. But what is the content of this truth Christians obey? Earlier, Peter defined that which Christians obey as being Jesus Christ himself: sanctified by the spirit for obedience to Jesus Christ (1:2). Truth, therefore, is God's own approach to life as revealed in his act of love for men in Jesus Christ. This event reveals the truth about our world and ourselves: "Jesus said to him, 'I am the way, and the truth, and the life'" (John 14:6).

The result of the holy and obedient life made possible by God's act in Jesus Christ is love. Therefore believers are to love one another earnestly from the heart. *Much of the remainder of I Peter calls believers to abandon those things which are inconsistent with the new life of love and to realize in their lives those things which belong to this new life.*

In these chapters on the life of love, I Peter also gives us one of the most beautiful passages ever written concerning the meaning of the church, a puzzling passage dealing with Christ's preaching to the spirits in prison, and a controversial reference to a fiery ordeal.

5

Commentary
on I Peter

Chapters 2—5

2:1-3 [1]So put away all malice and all guile and insincerity and envy and all slander. [2]Like newborn babes, long for the pure spiritual milk, that
by it you may grow up to salvation; [3]for you
have tasted the kindness of the Lord.

God's act has brought us to new birth. But what is
expected in the new life of love which is *man's response?*

According to the fairy tale, the wondrous change
worked in Cinderella's life by her fairy godmother was
largely a matter of a striking change in apparel. Man's

response to God likewise involves a striking change of apparel, but on a far deeper level. The ragged and soiled attitudes common to our world are to be stripped off (2:1) and the Christian is to clothe himself with an entirely new approach to life (cf. 5:5).

Put away all malice can be translated "strip off" all malice, for the Greek verb (*apothesthai*) can also be used to denote taking off clothing. This same verb occurs in similar advice to converts elsewhere in the New Testament, perhaps indicating that we are here dealing with a pattern of teaching regularly used in the membership classes of early Christianity. Compare the following verses which all contain the same verb and the same general picture:

. . . therefore *put away* all filthiness (James 1:21).

Let us then *cast off* the works of darkness and put on the armor of light . . . . Put on the Lord Jesus Christ (Rom. 13:12, 14).

But now *put* them all *away:* anger, wrath, malice, slander, and foul talk . . . . Put on then . . . compassion, kindness, lowliness . . . (Col. 3:8, 12).

Let us also *lay aside* every weight, and sin which clings so closely . . . (Heb. 12:1).

Christianity has so bound its message to the simplest acts of life that the most ordinary activities of the day serve as signs and reminders of Christian duty and experience. As we wash, we remember our baptism; as we eat, we are called to remember the covenant words spoken at the Lord's Supper; and even as we change clothing, we act out the Christian's stripping off the old way of life and putting on the garments of a new nature.

Malice (wickedness), guile (deception), insincerity (hypocrisy), envy, and slander (evil-speaking), all strike out against one's neighbor and thus betray the new life of love. They must therefore be stripped away. Note how often Jesus uses the words "no" and "do not" in the Sermon on the Mount. The Christian must learn to think negatively as well as positively, to say "no" to many prevalent attitudes and actions as well as "yes" to the new life of love.

From his adventures in the Yukon, Jack London observed that beginners on the Yukon trail attempted to carry with them all the conveniences belonging to their old way of life. Soon their packs grew too heavy and the sides of the trail were strewn with abandoned utensils. Those who refused to give up anything generally did not make it to the end of the trail. The Christian must also realize that, if he is to reach the goal of his pilgrimage, much belonging to the old life has to be abandoned.

Like newborn babes, long for the pure spiritual milk. The Christian will not only strip off the old ways, but will long for that which nourishes the new life. The Greek word *logikos*, here translated pure spiritual milk, could be translated "unadulterated milk of the word." The milk which nourishes the Christian could refer to the passage which tells of the word or good news through which the Christian has been born anew (1:22-25). The Christian knows that his new life depends as urgently upon his continuing contact with the good news of God's act which created him as does the life of a newborn babe upon its regular feedings. Without milk the baby soon dies, and without continuing nourishment through the gospel the new life of the Christian soon withers.

There is evidence that in early Christian practice, when new converts were baptized, they not only put on new clothing (white robes), but also were given milk to drink (perhaps with honey) and then joined in the Lord's Supper together. This section of I Peter may reflect such a scene in which the baptized exchange old clothing for new robes, join in the food of the new promised land (a land of "milk and honey"), and through Holy Communion become counted among those who have tasted the kindness of the Lord (cf. Ps. 34:8).

2:4-8 ⁴Come to him, to that living stone, rejected by men but in God's sight chosen and precious; ⁵and like living stones be yourselves built into a spiritual house, to be a holy priesthood . . . .

Although the word "church" does not appear in I Peter at all, this passage begins what is in fact one of the most beautiful and penetrating descriptions of the church in the New Testament.

The new life—begun by putting off the old nature and putting on the new, nourished by the gospel, and continued by growing up to salvation—is not lived in isolation. The new life of a Christian is "life together."

What is it that brings Christians together to form the church? Is it their attraction for one another or their organizational skill? No. It is that each is called to come to him, to that living stone. It was because each of the Twelve followed the same Galilean that all twelve found themselves in company with one another. Christians find themselves together when they find their way to Christ.

The description of Christ as that living stone derives from the early Christian interpretation of several Old Testament passages, including the interpretation by Christ himself of a passage in the Psalms:

> Jesus said: "Have you not read this scripture: 'The very stone which the builders rejected has become the head of the corner . . . '?"
>
> Mark 12:10 (quoting Ps. 118:22)

To this passage, I Peter links such verses as Isaiah 28:16, Isaiah 8:14-15, Exodus 19:6, Isaiah 43:20-21, and Hosea 1:6, 9 and 2:23:

> Therefore thus says the Lord GOD,
> "Behold, I am laying in Zion for a
> foundation
> a stone, a tested stone,
> a precious cornerstone, of a sure
> foundation:
> 'He who believes will not be in
> haste.' "
>
> Isaiah 28:16

> "And he will become a sanctuary, and a stone of offence, and a rock of stumbling to both houses of Israel, a trap and a snare to the inhabitants of Jerusalem. And many shall stumble thereon; they shall fall and be broken; they shall be snared and taken."
>
> Isaiah 8:14-15

"And you shall be to me a kingdom of priests
and a holy nation. These are the words which
you shall speak to the children of Israel."

Exodus 19:6

The wild beasts will honor me,
　the jackals and the ostriches;
for I give water in the wilderness,
　rivers in the desert,
to give drink to my chosen people,
　the people whom I have formed for myself
that they might declare my praise.

Isaiah 43:20-21

She conceived again and bore a daughter. And
the Lord said to him, "Call her name Not pitied,
for I will no more have pity on the house of
Israel, to forgive them at all. But I will have
pity on the house of Judah."

Hosea 1:6

And the Lord said, "Call his name Not my people, for you are not my people and I am not
your God."

Hosea 1:9

"And I will sow him for myself in the land.
And I will have pity on Not pitied,
　and I will say to Not my people,
　　'You are my people';
and he shall say, 'Thou art my God.'"

Hosea 2:23

The Old Testament was the Bible of the earliest
Christians and they believed that Christ himself was
the key to unlocking its meaning (cf. Luke 24:27, 32).
Prophetic passages which told of God's reestablish-
ment of his chosen people among the nations which
had rejected them were now interpreted as foretelling

the creation, through Jesus Christ, of a new nation of chosen people bound to God by a new covenant. No doubt early Christians shared with one another such lists of Old Testament passages which they believed were fulfilled and illuminated by the coming of Christ and the establishment of the new community of faith. So it is not surprising that some of the Old Testament passages quoted above to which I Peter refers are also used [in Acts 4:11, Romans 9:25-33, Ephesians 2:20-22, and elsewhere], to substantiate Christ's claim to messiahship and the truth of the gospel.

Those who come to that living stone become like living stones themselves.

In Beckett's play *Waiting for Godot,* when one of the characters points out a resemblance between himself and Jesus, his companion says in horror: "You're not going to compare yourself to Christ!" The first replies: "All my life I've compared myself to him." [1]

Comparing oneself to Christ is not blasphemy for the Christian; it is a necessity. The Christian is called to "put on the Lord Jesus Christ" (Rom. 13:14), to be "changed into his likeness" (II Cor. 3:18). Because Christ was a servant, the Christian is to be a servant (John 13:14-16); because Christ did great works, the Christian is to do great works (John 14:12). Similarly, because Christ is a living stone, Christians are to become like living stones which are built into a spiritual house.

Jesus was reported to have predicted the destruc-

[1] Samuel Beckett, *Waiting for Godot* (copyright, New York: Grove Press, 1954), p. 35.

tion of the Jerusalem temple (Matt. 24:2; Mark 14:58). He was also reported to have promised that he would build a new temple "not made with hands" (Mark 14:58; cf. John 2:19). I Peter seems to continue this line of thought. The old temple has passed away and Jesus himself is the foundation of a new temple. He builds a new spiritual house, employing as building material the very lives of his followers (cf. I Cor. 3:16-17). The special meeting place of God and man, once confined to Mount Zion, is no longer limited to one place but free, available to all through the living community of the redeemed. Wherever the redeemed gather in Christ's name, there is the spiritual house of God.

This picture of the redeemed as a living temple seems to suggest that Christians are also like those who serve within a temple, the holy priesthood (cf. Exod. 19:6; Rev. 5:10). As a member of a "priesthood of all believers" every Christian serves before God and offers up spiritual sacrifices (cf. Heb. 13:15). Instead of offering the old sacrifices of animals or produce, the Christian presents to God his entire life, the sum of his *being and doing*, as a living sacrifice (cf. Rom. 12:1).

The quotations from Isaiah, chapter 28, Psalm 118, and Isaiah, chapter 8, as joined together in I Peter (2:6-8), further reveal that even the rejection of Christ was foreseen by God. Nothing is beyond his knowledge and control; thus even disobedience may ultimately be made to work for the accomplishment of God's destined purpose.

2:9-10   ⁹But you are a chosen race, a royal priesthood, a holy nation, God's own people, that you may declare the wonderful deeds of him who called you out of darkness into his marvelous light. ¹⁰Once you were no people but now you are God's people; once you had not received mercy but now you have received mercy.

Here Peter's description of the church comes to its climax as several previous themes are brought together. Exodus 19:6, Isaiah 43:20-21, and Hosea, chapters 1 and 2 are now interwoven with the Old Testament passages already noted. The church is the new chosen people of God, a royal priesthood, a nation set apart for God's own purposes. The church is all these things, but not in order to tower majestically over the world. The church is all these things in order to become, like Christ, a humble, suffering servant in the world. Its service is to declare the wonderful deeds of him who called the church into existence.

How does the church declare God's wonderful deeds?

The church declares God's wonderful deeds by its very *being*. At the heart of God's deeds is his creation of a people, his building of believers as living stones into a spiritual house (2:5). The most public coming together of this spiritual house is the regular worship service. Christians who are able to attend cannot therefore in good conscience absent themselves from worship. One of their very reasons for existing is to form God's house in worship and thus proclaim to the neighborhood and world: See what God has done; from very ordinary people he has created an extraordinary house built upon and cemented together by his act of love in Jesus Christ! As each Christian takes his place in the house of living stones he proclaims: See, I believe in God's wonderful deeds! If anyone absents himself, there is a visible gap in God's house which fractures to some degree the declaration of God's deeds.

Besides declaring God's wonderful deeds by its very *being*, the church declares God's deeds by its *doing*. Sometimes this doing is a verbal defense of the Christian hope (3:15); sometimes it is reverent and chaste behavior which wins unbelievers without a word being spoken (3:1-2). Often it is the Christian's own good deeds which lead others to glorify God (2:12). Church life itself declares God's wonderful deeds through acts of mutual love and hospitality (4:8-9).

2:11-12   [11]Beloved, I beseech you as aliens and exiles to abstain from the passions of the flesh that wage war against your soul. [12]Maintain good conduct among the Gentiles, so that in case they speak against you as wrongdoers, they may see your good deeds and glorify God on the day of visitation.

With this passage Peter introduces a new section of his discourse which extends from chapter 2, verse 11 to chapter 3, verse 12. This entire section presents a practical working out of the believer's *response* to God's *act* through Christian social relationships in the world. It is *a Christian code of social ethics.*

Such codes of behavior have been given the title *Haustafeln* (house-tables) by German scholars. *Haustafeln* were popular among Jews and Greeks in the pagan world and quickly found their way into Christianity, transformed now by the Christian's understanding of life. Such summaries of proper *behavior* might be compared in a sense to a parent's final admonitions to a grown son or daughter about to leave for college. They carry advice on how one is to behave in the major relationships of life "out in the world." [1]

This Christian code of social ethics in I Peter 2:11 through 3:12 might be outlined:

1. Introduction   (2:11-12)
2. The Christian citizen   (2:13-17)
3. The Christian servant   (2:18-25)
4. The Christian wife   (3:1-6)
5. The Christian husband   (3:7)
6. Concluding advice   (3:8-12)

To this code compare Romans 13:1-7, Ephesians 5:21 through 6:9, Colossians 3:12 through 4:1, I Timothy 2:1-5, 6:1-2, and Titus 2:1 through 3:2. The very number of such *Haustafeln* in the New Testament should serve as a reminder of the importance given by the early church to man's response to God through Christian conduct in life's relationships.

1. *Christian behavior.* The introduction provided in 2:11-12 sets the general tenor of this code of ethics. The Christian's behavior is not determined by the world's customs but by the new life of God's kingdom;

---

[1] Compare Polonius's farewell to Laertes, *Hamlet*, Act I, Scene iii, ll. 59-82.

Christians are aliens and exiles in this world order (cf. 1:1, 1:17; Heb. 11:13). The Christian soldier "marches to a different drummer."

If his citizenship in God's new order is the key to *how* he is to act, what is the key to *why* he is to watch his behavior in this foreign world? The Christian maintains good conduct so that the earthbound may see your good deeds and glorify God (pp. 100 ff., 128 f.). The Christian's behavior is part of his active mission to the world. His daily conduct is a work of evangelism and can serve to bring new believers to birth.

The injunction that the Christian is to abstain from the passions of the flesh should not be interpreted as limiting sin to indulgence in smoking, drinking, or illicit sex. Peter uses flesh in the sense that Paul employs it in Romans 8:1-14 and Galatians 5:16-25. Here "flesh" connotes the entire human being who, when he is alienated from God, lives in bondage to the "original sin" of self-centeredness which fights to control the direction of our life from birth onward. Sins of the flesh therefore include not only licentiousness and drunkenness, but also "strife, jealousy, anger, selfishness, dissension, party spirit, envy" (Gal. 5:20-21).

2:13-17   13Be subject for the Lord's sake to every human institution, whether it be to the emperor as supreme, 14or to governors as sent by him . . . .

2. *The Christian citizen.* The Christian is to do what the man of flesh hates to do, to put on humility and subject himself to the authority invested in others.

I Peter is closer to Paul's view of the Christian's relationship to the State (cf. Romans, Chapter 13) than to the Book of Revelation which sometimes lashes out in anger against Rome. Unlike Romans 13, however, I Peter does not speak of the "divine right" of governmental rulers. Apparently the ignorance of foolish men needed to be silenced by the display of Christian obedience and good citizenship. Pagan neighbors may well have been suspicious of the new converts' transformed way of life because of their refusal to join in the old gossiping and pagan celebrations of the neighborhood (cf. 4:4). To be "different" often means to be labeled "unpatriotic," "seditious," or to be accused of all manner of hideous, hidden crimes. Many wild charges were thus brought against the Christians. The Roman historian Tacitus, for example, refers to Christians as "a class hated for their abominations," and notes that in Nero's time Christians were convicted of "hatred against mankind." Exemplary citizenship on the part of Christians is demanded in order to silence these malicious rumors and unfounded attacks. The Christian's service is freely volunteered, not grudgingly rendered in cringing servility. Christians are free men with regard to the "conflicting interests" of the world because they are owned as servants (slaves) of God.

Verse 17 goes beyond the immediate context and serves as a brilliant summary statement of Christian ethics: Honor all men. Love the brotherhood. Fear God. Honor the emperor. The Christian sees the value of every human personality. This honoring of all men takes on a special quality in the brotherhood, for these believers have learned to share as a family in Christian love. God's awesome power and holiness are recognized in reverent fear. The emperor is to receive honor as a man invested with authority for keeping order.

2:18-25   ¹⁸Servants, be submissive to your masters with all respect . . . ²⁰if when you do right and suffer for it you take it patiently, you have God's approval. ²¹For to this you have been called, because Christ also suffered for you, leaving you an example, that you should follow in his steps . . . .

3. *The Christian servant.* The word translated servants in this passage is actually the word *oiketai* which means "slaves," particularly the slaves of the *oikos* or "household." A wealthy family might own tutors, bookkeepers, managers, and artists, as well as domestics and manual laborers. A surprisingly large percentage of the workers in the ancient world were actually slaves, and certainly a large proportion of the early Christian members would have belonged to this class. From these Christian workers Peter calls for humble submissiveness to their masters. The Christian worker is to show respect and do right in his work. He is neither to nurse hatred and resentment nor to encourage rebellion and bloodshed, but must be willing to suffer patiently even when punished unjustly.

This does not mean that the Christian cannot speak to the authorities on behalf of the truth (cf. 3:15) or even disobey the one in power if his commands contradict God's word (cf. Acts 4:19-20). But in such cases the Christian is to speak with gentleness and reverence (3:15), and be prepared to suffer for his convictions.

The Christian's willingness to submit to unjustified suffering conforms to the pattern set by Christ himself as the "suffering servant." I Peter quotes or paraphrases Isaiah's description of the "suffering servant" (Isa. 53), setting forth the example left by Christ: no guile was found on his lips (cf. Isa. 53:9) . . . . He himself bore our sins (cf. Isa. 53:4, 12) . . . . By his wounds you have been healed (cf. Isa. 53:5).

The heart of this passage goes far beyond advice to servants in relation to their masters; it is a key to the whole of the Christian life: Christ has left an example, that you should follow in his steps. The Christian life is a pilgrimage in his steps. In spite of the many differences between the Christian world of the first century and our world today, there is still a legitimate place in our life for the question, "What would Jesus do?"

The Greek word *hupogrammon,* translated example in this passage, is worthy of special note. It originally signified a *tracing tablet* on which were letters a child copied in learning the alphabet, or an *architect's drawing* or *artist's sketch* the details of which were to be followed or filled in by others. In his use of this term Peter is saying that Christ has left us such a pattern or plan which we must retrace as a child traces the perfect lettering of his teacher, a blueprint which we must follow if we are to build our lives according to Christ's design, a sketch we must fill out in our daily living.

The final verse of this passage, verse 25, describes the believers as sheep who were once straying but have now returned to the shepherd and guardian of souls. God is spoken of as a shepherd in such passages as Psalm 23 and Isaiah 40:11, and the term is applied to Jesus in Mark 6:34, John 10:11-16, I Peter 5:4, and elsewhere. The word for guardian (*episkopos*) might also be translated "overseer," and finally comes to be the title "bishop."

3:1-7 ¹Likewise you wives, be submissive to your husbands.... ⁷Likewise you husbands, live considerately with your wives....

4. *The Christian wife.* I Peter's advice to wives seems to be directed particularly to Christian women married to non-Christian husbands (cf. I Cor. 7:12-16).

The wife is to be submissive, reverent, and chaste. By such conduct, Peter reasons hopefully, some husbands may be won without a word by the behavior of their wives. Thus the writer of the epistle records his belief that Christian attitudes and acts can greatly influence unbelievers.

Such evangelism by act and attitude may be of special significance in our own day. Words have become devaluated in our billboard-radio-TV civilization in which questionable claims and counterclaims fill the air constantly. Does the voice of the Christian speak with greater validity than the thousands of voices around us that sound so sincere as they attempt to sell hundreds of thousands of products and prejudices? Today there may be more need than ever for the witness of the quiet deed and unpretentious attitude, for the Good Samaritan who simply performs an act of mercy without trying to sell a bill of goods. A world that has witnessed and been moved by such an act of love, with no strings attached, will be surprised enough to ask the reason for such an act and sufficiently ingenious to discover the answer. Perhaps the longing of our modern world is well expressed in those oft-used words, "I'd rather see a sermon any day, than hear one."

In a beautiful passage I Peter advises wives to refrain from undue attention to outward adorning, and calls upon the Christian wife to attend rather to the hidden person of the heart with the imperishable jewel of a gentle and quiet spirit. He directs attention to Sarah, wife of Abraham, whose submissiveness and deference to her husband serve as examples to the Christian wife.

5. *The Christian husband.* Christian husbands are advised to live considerately with [their] wives, bestowing honor on the woman as the weaker sex. One might compare this attitude with Paul's view that special honor is to be given to the weaker parts of the church as the body of Christ (I Cor. 12:23 ff.). Though women are spoken of as the weaker sex, wives have no less a share in the grace of the new life in Christ than do husbands; together husband and wife are joint heirs of the grace of life. The Christian's relationship within the family and his relationship to God

are bound together. If the husband does not relate himself as a Christian to his wife, his relationship to God is also likely to be broken; his prayers will be hindered.

3:8-12 [8]Finally, all of you, have unity of spirit, sympathy, love of the brethren, a tender heart and a humble mind. [9]Do not return evil for evil or reviling for reviling . . . .

6. *Concluding advice*. With these words summarizing the qualities of a Christian life, to which is added a supporting quotation from Psalm 34, I Peter concludes this Christian code of social ethics.

While most of the qualities of life mentioned here have already been remarked upon, we might take special note of the exhortation that Christians should not return evil for evil or reviling for reviling.

Some years ago a popular magazine displayed on its cover a series of pictures which showed a boss yelling at one of his employees, the employee returning home and yelling at his wife, the wife yelling at their little boy, and the little boy finally yelling at his dog. Ill will, reviling, or evil often sets off chain reactions in our world, moving in vicious circles and leaving behind swathes of destruction which generate further cycles of ill will.

How is one ever to stop the gathering momentum of such evil? I Peter's answer is that the chain reaction or vicious cycle of evil and reviling should end at the Christian's door. God has called upon Christians to absorb the world's evil and reviling and to bless in return, thus breaking the chain of destruction or cycle of ill will. To counteract ill will with blessing is not easy, but it is possible for the disciple who traces out in his living the life of his Lord. The Christian then, like his Lord, bears the sins of the world, heals others through the wounds he receives, and himself receives a blessing.

3:13-17   [13]Now who is there to harm you if you are zealous for what is right? [14]But even if you do suffer for righteousness' sake, you will be blessed. . . . [15]Always be prepared to make a defense to any one who calls you to account for the hope that is in you, . . .

Several thoughts from the previous Christian code of social ethics are continued here, though now with special emphasis upon the blessing which accompanies Christlike suffering. Perhaps Jesus' own words lie behind this teaching:

Blessed are those who are persecuted for righteousness' sake, for theirs is the kingdom of heaven.

Matt. 5:10

The call to good behavior is again repeated, and the Christian is further exhorted to be ready and willing to make a fearless defense to any one who calls you to account for the hope that is in you. This defense, however, is not to be proud and provocative, as if courting martyrdom, but is to be made with gentleness and reverence. Perhaps Christians were already being dragged before the Roman courts by suspicious neighbors, "witch-hunting" crowds, or an occasional

138

sadistic official. The Christian was to state his beliefs openly, fearlessly, yet humbly.

Such advice is applicable today. Too often Christians enter the arena of public debate with a chip on the shoulder, assuming that any who dare question a Christian doctrine are enemies unworthy of a civil answer, let alone a gentle and reverent answer. At times an antagonistic and self-righteous attitude prevails even within the visitation programs of the church itself. Such attitudes can lead to the use of campaign tricks and pressure tactics which may seem to assure the year's budget or to win a record number of new members, but may well be building up the life of an organization at the cost of tearing down the life of the church. It seems obvious that as our collection of sales gimmicks has increased, the spiritual influence of the church has decreased. In the long run, it is good behavior in Christ and gentleness and reverence in discourse which convey the gospel to the world.

3:18-22   [18]For Christ . . . [19]went and preached to the spirits in prison, [20]who formerly did not obey, when God's patience waited in the days of Noah, during the building of the ark, in which a few, that is, eight persons, were saved through water. [21]Baptism, which corresponds to this, now saves you . . . .

We come now to a vague and puzzling reference to Christ's having preached to the spirits in prison (3: 19), and to what may seem a rather surprising comparison of Christian baptism to the great flood and Noah's ark (3:20-22).

While continuing the previous discussion concerning Christian suffering, verse 18 now emphasizes the centrality of Christ's own suffering and death as both the Christian's salvation and example. But what connection and what particular meaning has the following reference to spirits in prison and the days of Noah?

Scholars have a variety of suggestions and interpretations. Some suggest that verses 18-22 are really part of an early Christian hymn which was incorporated here. Taken out of the original context, these few lines might well be puzzling to us. Some have suggested that verse 19 originally told of Enoch or Noah rather than Christ visiting the spirits in prison, but that the name Enoch or Noah was somehow dropped out of the text. We do know that a Jewish writing known as I Enoch mentions that the patriarch Enoch (cf. Gen. 5:21-24) appeared to imprisoned spirits, these spirits perhaps to be identified with the "fallen angels" mentioned in Genesis 6:2, 4. That the book of I Enoch was known and valued by Christians is indicated by reference to it in Jude, verses 14-15, while popular Christian speculation concerning the fallen angels and Noah's day is indicated in II Peter 2:4-5.[1]

The scholar Bo Reicke has suggested another line of interpretation which may better explain this passage.[2]

---

[1] See "Exegesis" and "Exposition," *The Interpreter's Bible*, Vol. XII, pp. 132-133.
[2] Bo Reicke, *The Disobedient Spirits and Christian Baptism: A Study of I Peter 3:19 and Its Context* (Copenhagen: Munksgaard,

I Peter had exhorted Christians to speak fearlessly in defense of the Christian hope when called to account, probably before pagan courts, crowds, or magistrates.

But how could Christians, who were poor and ordinary folk, appear before the heathen powers of the day without fear (3:14)? Here Christ's preaching to the spirits in prison is introduced. Again Christ is the great example. Fearlessly he provided the pattern for Christians by descending between the time of his death and resurrection into the realm of the dead.[3] Probably the spirits in prison refers to an early Jewish belief that the "fallen angels" (Gen. 6:2; II Peter 2:4-5) and their offspring, as well as the other great sinners of Noah's day, were imprisoned in the underworld. In a sense these evil ones who provoked the great flood were viewed as the patrons and powers behind the heathen nations of the believers' own day. If Christ preached fearlessly to such great sinners, Christians should be able to imitate him in defending the faith fearlessly before the pagans who opposed or accused them.

But this passage implies more than this. If Christ carried the gospel even to those ancients whose disregard of God's authority lay at the very root of the origin of heathenism, and yet rose victorious in resurrection, the hidden power of heathenism can be

---

1946). Compare the same scholar's comments in *The Epistles of James, Peter, and Jude,* The Anchor Bible, Vol. 37 (Garden City, N.Y.: Doubleday and Co., Inc., 1964), pp. 106 ff.

[3] Note that in some traditions the words "He descended into hell" appear in the Apostles' Creed.

broken. The Christian can stand before heathens knowing that Christ has already taken from them any ultimate power. "He disarmed the principalities and powers and made a public example of them, triumphing over them in him" (Col. 2:15).

Aside from the Jewish-Christian speculation concerning the underworld which is involved, this puzzling discussion carries an important truth concerning the universality of the gospel and Christ's power (cf. Eph. 4:8-10). There is no place where Christ cannot make himself known. There are no limits to the gospel. Christ has already cut the root of evil. The Christian need not fear when trials come, for they are only evil's death throes. Christ's final victory over all things including the hidden realms of sin and death is already assured, and his people will share in this victory. Thus medieval art could picture the realm of sin and death as a great monster, but, standing in the open mouth of that now defeated monster, was Christ, leading Adam and Eve out to freedom.

The connection between I Peter's reference to Christ's death and his preaching to the spirits in prison (3:18-19) and the following comparison of baptism to the flood and Noah's ark (3:20-22) becomes clear when we remember that not only did Christ speak of his suffering and death as a baptism (cf. Mark 10:38; Luke 12:50), but that baptism was in fact pictured as an actual participation by believers in the death and resurrection of Christ. At baptism one died to the old way of life and was born into the new resurrection-life. Paul could write:

Do you not know that all of us who have been baptized into Christ Jesus were baptized into his death? We were buried therefore with him by baptism into death, so that as Christ was raised from the dead by the glory of the Father, we too might walk in newness of life (Rom. 6:3-4).

Thus Christ's death and his bringing of the gospel to the evildoers of Noah's day suggests the Christian's participation in Christ's death and the triumph through baptism over the convert's own evil tendencies. Further, the great flood, which the evildoers of Noah's day provoked, serves as a parallel or "type" of Christian baptism. Just as the flood marked the death of the old world and the birth of the new through the survival of Noah and his family on the ark, so baptism marks the end of the old creation and the beginning of a new creation through the salvation of the newborn converts. The church then might be compared to Noah's ark. It is a haven of refuge in a stormy world, a sign of salvation and God's gift of a new beginning for humanity. The number on the ark, eight persons,[1] may signify perfection or wholeness in I Peter, for, since the number seven was regarded as sacred, the addition of one to the sacred number might cap the climax. This entire passage takes on a special significance if we accept the view that we are dealing here with a baptismal sermon, preached after the performance of the ceremony, reminding the converts of the crucial meaning of the sacrament in which they had just participated.

---

[1] Noah, his wife, his three sons, and their wives (Gen. 7:13).

4:1-6 ¹Since therefore Christ suffered in the flesh, arm yourselves with the same thought . . . . ³Let the time that is past suffice for doing what the Gentiles like to do, living in licentiousness, . . .

We have compared I Peter to a rich tapestry dominated by two major motifs, *God's act* and *man's response*. If one looks carefully at this tapestry, he will note that a certain underlying pattern involving these two motifs is repeated over and over again with varying colors or emphases. Thus this passage, although it gives special emphasis to suffering, also involves a design we have encountered earlier. *Events in Christ's life make available to the believer both a new life freed from the sins of the past and an example to be followed.* This pattern has already occurred, for example, in 1:3-15, 1:18 through 2:4, and 2:6-12.

Christ's passion, referred to now in 4:1, offers to the believer both a new life and an example. Believers are to arm themselves with the same thought (or mind) displayed by Christ in his passion (cf. Phil. 2:5). Whoever traces in his own life the pattern of Christ's suffering shares in Christ's dying and thus also shares the new life of the risen Christ (cf. Rom. 6:8). This birth to a new mode of life allows the believer to strip off sin and the old tyranny of human passions and live now by the will of God (cf. I Peter 4:1-2).

At this point I Peter (4:2) provides a catalogue of the sins the new converts in Asia Minor had stripped off in becoming baptized Christians. Similar catalogues of the vices of paganism occur in Romans (1:28-32),

Galatians (5:19-21), Ephesians (5:3-5), and elsewhere. No doubt the vices listed in I Peter were common to certain of the fertility-centered cults and popular clubs or associations of Asia Minor. The pagan participants were surprised that their one-time companions did not now join them in these popular celebrations. Because the new converts had broken with the locally accepted customs, the townsfolk abused them.

Abuse for refusing to join in popularly supported customs can be a source of very real suffering. The Jews have suffered almost constant harassment and sometimes terrible butcherings as the price for allowing their religion to set them apart from local customs. Stories of recent martyrs, slain because of their refusal to accept local racial customs, will remain etched on the minds of many in this generation. The questioning of popularly accepted answers to the problems of war and peace may lead to the questioner's being branded a Communist sympathizer, and lead to the destruction of his reputation, loss of his job, and disruption of his family. One who criticizes the crowd's disdain for speed limits and traffic regulations may be called a coward. The person who feels compelled to favor a needed mental-health clinic over a popular stadium construction project, a mission church school over gold candlesticks or a new church kitchen, may suffer more subtle forms of abuse for his opposition to the opinion of the majority or the preference of power cliques.

Christians should not be surprised (4:12) that they

are called upon to bear abuse and suffering; for, from the beginning, the same experience of suffering has been required of your brotherhood throughout the world (5:9). The Christian ought rather to worry if he is never abused and never caused to suffer, for that may well be a sign that he has surprised no one at all with a new way of life because he simply conforms to the tyranny of public opinion.

I Peter advises Christians when they are abused to remember that the abusers and the abused will all give account to him who is ready to judge the living and the dead (4:5). This reference to the all-inclusiveness of the judgment leads Peter to announce that the gospel has already been preached even to the dead. Thus even those who died before Christ's coming have been given the opportunity to live in the spirit (4:6).

4:7-11   [7]The end of all things is at hand; therefore keep sane and sober for your prayers. [8]Above all hold unfailing your love for one another, since love covers a multitude of sins. [9]Practice hospitality . . . . As each has received a gift, employ it for one another, . . .

Having catalogued the old sins which have been stripped off, I Peter now turns attention to the acts and attitudes which should clothe the new life lived in expectation of the coming judgment. Paul similarly followed his list of "the works of the flesh" with a list of the "fruit of the Spirit" (Gal. 5:19-23).

How is the church to live in this critical time when

the end of all things is at hand? Sustained and directed through its prayers, it is to avoid hysteria. Its members are to hold unfailing their love for one another, practice hospitality, and employ their various talents for the upbuilding of one another. The total activity of the Christian community should be so directed that God may be glorified through Jesus Christ.

There have been some arguments concerning the meaning of the words in verse 8, love covers a multitude of sins (cf. Prov. 10:12; James 5:20). Whose sins are covered, those of the one loving or the one being loved? Probably this question did not occur to the writer. Rather than thinking of love as whitewash which covers sinful lives, he would seem to be emphasizing the unifying power of Christian love.[1] Christian love so binds us together in Christ that evil tendencies are quickly recognized and weeded out. The Gospel of John speaks of such love as being the very sign by which the world will recognize true disciples: "By this all men will know that you are my disciples, if you have love for one another" (John 13:35).

On the Christian use of gifts discussed in verses 10-11, compare Romans 12:3-13 and I Corinthians 12:4-31. The words grace (*charis*) and gift (*charisma*) which appear together here have closely related meanings in Greek. Hence all our gifts are evidences of God's varied grace.

Verse 11 concludes this section with a doxology:

---

[1] In Luke 7:47 Jesus associates love and forgiveness. To the one who loves much, much is forgiven, and likewise the one who is forgiven little, loves little.

To him belong glory and dominion for ever and ever. Compare the similar doxology in Romans 16:27 and in the doxology we attach to the end of the Lord's Prayer.

4:12-19   [12]Beloved, do not be surprised at the fiery ordeal which comes upon you to prove you, as though something strange were happening to you. [13]But rejoice in so far as you share Christ's sufferings, . . .

I Peter now speaks of the fiery ordeal which comes upon the readers. He seems to picture them in the midst of present persecution. As we noted earlier, this reference to the presence of a fiery ordeal has been explained by some as a shift in I Peter from an incorporated baptismal sermon to remarks written specificially for readers undergoing persecution in Asia Minor. Others believe news of an outbreak of persecution reached the author just before he began writing verse 12 of chapter 4. Still others, however, point out that the entire letter of I Peter has dealt with *suffering for the faith*. Perhaps, as the author comes to the end of his letter, he is simply attempting to make it clearer than ever that he intends his message to speak to those who are experiencing a very real fiery ordeal. This fiery ordeal may not mean official or full-scale persecution of all Christians. I Peter has already employed the image of fire to describe the testing of faith through various trials (1:6), and has referred to abuse by pagan neighbors (4:4) and perhaps occasional trials before pagan courts (cf. our comments on I James 3:15, 19-20, pp. 138-39, 142.)

I Peter makes a number of points concerning the Christian and suffering: (1) Christians should not be surprised that they meet with sufferings; (2) persecution is a testing (to prove you); (3) Christians share (or fellowship in) Christ's sufferings; (4) this sharing should lead the Christian to rejoice; (5) one must not assume that all suffering is suffering as a Christian; and (6) persecution is a sign that God's final judgment is beginning (cf. Mark 13:8-13).

We have already discussed the meaning of trials in the Christian life (cf. comments on James 1:2) and the example of Christ's own suffering as the pattern for the Christian to follow (cf. comments on I Pet. 2:20 ff., 3:14 ff. pp. 133-34, 138). Certainly suffering should be no surprise: "If they persecuted me, they will persecute you also" (John 15:20). And certainly sharing in the very pattern of Christ's life, painful though it may sometimes be, includes joy: "Then they left the presence of the council, rejoicing that they were counted worthy to suffer dishonor for the name" (Acts 5:41).

Some scholars, such as John Wick Bowman and Bo Reicke, suggest that the warning that none of you suffer as a murderer . . . or a mischief-maker (verse 15) may be particularly aimed at the militant nationalistic movement of the day which sought to provoke open battle with Rome through acts of terrorism. To suffer innocently for Christian faith is not the same as to incur punishment for Zealot terrorism.

In our day we need this same warning that not all

suffering is to be counted suffering as a Christian. Not only are we all too willing to interpret the least inconvenience as a cross which we voluntarily and nobly carry, but we seek to account for the disasters which come as a result of our pride, greed, and envy as though they were sufferings for Christ. Whenever we are inclined to "play the martyr" we might well suspect that we are not suffering at all as a Christian.

The word Christian (*Christianos*) is rare in the New Testament, occurring only here (v. 16) and in Acts 11:26 and 26:28. It seems that only outsiders called the early believers "Christians," while the believers themselves preferred such self-descriptions as "disciples," "saints," "brothers," or "followers of the way."

5:1-5   ¹So I exhort the elders among you, as a fellow elder and a witness of the sufferings of Christ . . . . ²Tend the flock of God that is your charge, not by constraint but willingly, . . . ⁴and when the chief Shepherd is manifested you will obtain the unfading crown of glory. . . .

The author, about to conclude his letter, directs some closing words of advice and encouragement to various groups within the readers' community. His words to the elders who tend the flock seem especially timely, as good leadership would be vital in a time of fiery ordeal.

If Simon Peter himself stands behind these words, it is noteworthy that he humbly identifies himself with all who perform pastoral duties; he is a fellow

elder. The word elder (*presbuteros*) or "presbyter" referred to leading men in the Jewish community (cf. Mark 8:31), and was borrowed by the Christian church to designate its own leaders (Acts 14:23; I Tim. 5:17, etc.).

Peter can also refer to himself as a witness of the sufferings of Christ. Just as the title apostle called attention not to Peter but to the one who sent him (cf. comments on 1:1), so the present description focuses not upon Peter but upon Christ. The word witness is actually the Greek word *martus* (martyr), later restricted to designate one who witnesses to Christ by giving up his life.

The words "pastor" and "pastoral" are the Latin equivalents of our Anglo-Saxon words "shepherd" and "shepherding" and are used today by the church to designate its clergy and their work in tending the needs of the laity. In the Old Testament the terms "shepherd" and "flock" are applied to a leader and his people (II Sam. 5:2) and especially to God and Israel (Ps. 23; Isa. 40:11). The New Testament uses this imagery in speaking of Christ and his followers and of Christian leaders and the community of believers (John 21:15-17; Acts 20:28-29). Christian shepherds, in imitation of Christ, give themselves willingly and eagerly to their task. Their authority is not that of a domineering spirit, but is the very authority emphasized so often by I Peter in relation to Christ, the authority of example. The coming appearance of Christ himself, who is now called the chief Shepherd (cf. 2:25), will reward those who have followed his pattern of shepherding with a crown of glory woven of amaranth, a flower which was believed to be unfading (cf. our comments on "crown," James 1:12, pp. 39-40).[1]

The author then turns to advise another group in the community, the younger followers. They are to put on the clothing of humility (cf. 3:8) in relation to one another and especially to be subject to the elders who are their shepherds in the faith.

5:6-11   [6]Humble yourselves therefore under the mighty hand of God, that in due time he may exalt you. [7]Cast all your anxieties on him, for he cares about you. [8]Be sober, be watchful. . . . [10]And after you have suffered a little while, the God of all grace, who has called you to his eternal glory in Christ, will himself restore, establish, and strengthen you. [11]To him be the dominion for ever and ever. Amen.

The author's final words of advice and encouragement continue the theme of humility, adding an assurance of God's care, a call to watchfulness and steadfastness, and a closing doxology.

Believers should be moved to humble themselves under the mighty hand of God which exalts the lowly, takes up the anxieties of those who trust him, and

---

[1] There is an interesting passage on the "crown of glory" in the "Exegesis," *The Interpreter's Bible*, Vol. XII, pp. 150-51.

will finally restore, establish, and strengthen the steadfast.

The simplicity of verse 7 with its picture of God
as the one who cares about our individual lives is
particularly beautiful: Cast all your anxieties on him,
for he cares about you. These words call to mind
Jesus' own teaching reported in Matthew 6:25-34.

The theme of suffering, introduced in 1:6 and
woven throughout the text of I Peter appears also
in this closing exhortation. Peter does not describe
the Christian life as a pleasant walk on a primrose
path. Your adversary the devil prowls around like a
roaring lion, seeking some one to devour (v. 8). The
readers in Asia Minor are not the only ones threat-
ened, however, for the same experience of suffering
is required of the brotherhood throughout the world.
No doubt the abuse of pagan neighbors, trials in
pagan law courts, and the fiery ordeal mentioned
earlier are all seen as the work of the prowling forces
of evil in the world. The Christian therefore must be
watchful, willing to resist evil, and firm in faith. Beyond this little while of suffering lies eternal glory in
Christ.

5:12-14 12By Silvanus, a faithful brother as I regard
him, I have written briefly to you, exhorting
and declaring that this is the true grace of
God; stand fast in it. 13She who is at Babylon, who is likewise chosen, sends you greetings; and so does my son Mark. 14Greet one
another with the kiss of love.

Peace to all of you that are in Christ.

Perhaps Peter takes the pen in hand himself to add these closing greetings (cf. Gal. 6:11; II Thess. 3:17) and to acknowledge that it is by Silvanus, a faithful brother, that he has written this letter. In our discussion of the first verse of the letter we noted that Silvanus is no doubt another name for Silas. (See pages 97-8.)

The writer adds that she who is at Babylon sends greetings to the likewise chosen Christians of Asia Minor, the readers. Christian writers depicted Rome as the contemporary Babylon. Like ancient Babylon, Rome was mistress of the pagan world (Rev. 14:8; 16:19).

Mark, who also sends them greetings, is very possibly John Mark, the relative of Barnabas (Col. 4:10) who shared part of the first missionary journey with Paul (Acts 12:25; 15:39), and who is later mentioned in Philemon 24. According to tradition, John Mark later became "the interpreter of Peter" and author of the Gospel of Mark.[1]

As he weaves the last threads into his tapestry, the author holds the full design up to view. He has woven together declaration and exhortation, the act of God and the response of man: I have written briefly to you, exhorting and declaring that this is the true grace of God; stand fast in it. The declaring of God's true grace is answered by a discipleship which will stand fast in it. *God's gracious act is to be answered by man's obedient response.* This new life of obedi-

---

[1] See I Peter, "Exegesis" and "Exposition," *The Interpreter's Bible*, Vol. XII, pp. 158-59.

ence is clothed with a courage which finds hope and joy even in suffering.

The kiss of love was apparently a greeting practiced in Judaism (cf. Luke 7:45). It now becomes a sign of the mutual love within the Christian fellowship (cf. Rom. 16:16). As we have seen, the word peace likewise comes from Judaism where it was and continues to be used as a word of greeting and parting. Peter, who began this letter with the prayer that Christians increasingly share in the wholeness and harmony of salvation which is peace, now concludes with the similar benediction: Peace to all of you that are in Christ.

6

Christian Being and Doing
A Summing Up

What can we say concerning this Bible study we have engaged in together?

An Expedition. Perhaps, as suggested earlier, it has in some ways resembled a mountain-climbing expedition. Some have probably discovered new muscles on the climb, mental and spiritual muscles whose aches now remind them that they have been exercised all too little in the past. All, possibly, may have found some ascents steep and difficult, beset by obstacles which have caused them to stumble and to break the best of intentions. Such stumblings are not disastrous if we are willing to get to our feet again and continue the climb. Those who have climbed with a group, bound to one another, have surely been gratified by the invaluable assistance one climber can give another. Some have been rewarded with an occasional clear view of the landscape below, offering a new perspective of the world in which we live. Through this climb some perhaps have gained the confidence and encouragement to try other peaks of this mountain range we call the Bible.

A Personal Message. Perhaps, as we anticipated at the outset, some have found that James and I Peter are not merely interesting translations of ancient essays. They may have discovered that these two letters bore their own names and addresses and were indeed written to them personally by members of their own family of faith concerning the meaning and purpose of life itself. Such messages may have brought about a transformation in the lives of some readers, converting them to a new seriousness in *Christian doing*, unfolding to them a new dimension in *Christian being*. Certainly James and I Peter will not have spoken so directly to all, very likely only to a few, "For the gate is narrow and the way is hard that leads to life, and those who find it are few" (Matt. 7:14).

Let us conclude with a word of summary about each of the two books of our study.

CHRISTIAN DOING IN JAMES

Søren Kierkegaard, living in a day when it was popular for every person to consider himself a Christian, heard many excusing themselves from living Christian lives by complaining that there were so many "obscure passages" in the Bible that one was at a loss to know how one really ought to act. Kierkegaard answered that he would take this excuse seriously only if the speaker's life showed that he "scrupulously observed all the passages which are easy to understand." [1]

The peculiar power of the Book of James resides in the "easy to understand" nature of its commands to obedience. It would be exceedingly difficult to plead that one could not understand James' warnings against the malicious use of the tongue (James 1:26 and 3:6) or his attack upon favoritism for the rich and powerful over the poor and helpless (2:1-8). Likewise, James' call to joy in trials (1:2, 12) and to a faith that works in the world can hardly be called obscure. James' directness disarms us, uncovers those sins we refuse to acknowledge, and commands us to obedience in the ordinary situations of life.

Earlier we described the Book of James as a Christian Wisdom Book written by a Jewish-Christian teacher to the early church in a time of moral crisis. Perhaps James is especially appropriate for our day as we face a similar moral crisis in which professions of faith all too often fail to issue in works of love. James, once called an "epistle of straw," may be the "epistle of rock" intended to shatter our comfortable

---

[1] *For Self-Examination*. Trans. by Edna and Howard Hong (Minneapolis: Augsburg Publishing House, 1940), p. 29.

illusion that discipleship makes no sacrificial claims upon us in the large issues or little honesties of life.

What have we found to be the heart of the Book of James? The words of James 1:2-4 which call the believer in time of crisis and trials to a mature or grown-up discipleship. What has halted the disciple's growth? The false assumption that one can have faith without works, the name "Christian" without the life of obedience (1:22 ff.; 2:14 ff.).

Though there is much else in James, including an often overlooked emphasis upon faith and quiet receptivity (cf. 1:6, 21), this little book works its purpose as it disturbs us and refuses to allow us to live in peace with a faith that has no works, with a barren and hypocritical "Christianity" that seeks to exist without obedience, sacrifice, or cross.

Mark Twain once observed that whereas many people were bothered by the parts of the Bible they couldn't understand, he was bothered most by the parts of the Bible he could understand.

The purpose of James in our day might well be to "bother" us with clearly understandable demands. The Christian and the church deserve to lose some sleep over easy compromises with "the way things are" and "the way things are done" in this world. The beginning of our cure may well be a goading pain that will not let us rest while there remains a terrible gulf between creed and act, between claim to believe and will to do, between the name Christian and the obedient life of the grown-up disciple.

In one of his poems E. E. Cummings writes of "the Cambridge ladies who live in furnished souls . . . ." He observes that these well-bred, pious ladies, probably regarded as pillars of their church, ". . . believe in Christ and Longfellow, both dead . . . ."[1]

Can it be that Cummings' shaft has struck the very heart of the moral crisis of our day? Is it not true that, even in the church, many attempt to "live in furnished souls," to "decorate" their lives with a religion designed by others, according to popular taste, without attempting to achieve a purpose—an authentic, firsthand Christian environment of their own?

How is it that often church members content themselves with borrowed ideas and beliefs, with "furnished souls"? Cummings has the key to these second-hand pseudo-Christians. They "believe in Christ and Longfellow, both dead." If God's special act of love is nothing more than an event in the historic past and Christ an interesting figure, who, like Longfellow, lived and died and was buried, then the Christian ethic—Christian action—is like a tree severed from its root, destined to perish like the flower of the field, and "Christians" are living on, blindly copying the long dead forms and rituals of a bygone day.

James calls the disciple to *Christian doing;* I Peter reminds us that *Christian doing* takes place where there is vital *Christian being.*

---

[1] From "Sonnets—Realities" (I) in *Tulips and Chimneys* (E. E. Cummings, *Poems 1923-1954* [New York: Harcourt, Brace and Company, 1954], p. 58).

I Peter affirms that our birth to a new and vital way of life springs from our association with a living Christ (cf. I Pet. 1:3). It is because there is the "good news" of a reconciling God that we therefore gird up [our] minds . . . (cf. 1:12-13; 1:25 through 2:1).

Earlier we described I Peter as a rich tapestry dominated by two major motifs: God's act (the gospel); and man's response (the Christian life). It is at the point where God's act and man's response meet that *Christian being* comes to birth and a life of *Christian doing* results. I Peter makes clear that it is God's act of mercy which moves man to respond in a new life of joyful obedience.

Interwoven with these major motifs are many other basic Christian affirmations. Baptism, the sacrament which marks the birth of *Christian being*, has a vital place in this tapestry (cf. 3:21), for, as we have seen, I Peter may in fact embody an early Christian baptismal sermon (1:3 through 4:11).

Adding to the rich pattern of I Peter's message are his call to a share in Christ's sufferings (cf. 1:6; 4:1 ff.; 4:12 ff.), his code of Christian social ethics (2:11 through 3:12), a paralleling of the history of the New Covenant to the Old (cf. our comments on 1:1-2), and a description of salvation as so all-embracing that it reaches even the spirits in prison (3:18-19; 4:6). Coloring the warp and woof of the tapestry are a series of similes depicting the Christian community, the church, as dispersed exiles (1:1; 2:11), newborn children (1:14; 2:2), a house of living stones (2:4-8), a chosen race and royal priesthood (2:9), and the flock guarded by elders and the chief Shepherd (5:1 ff.).

Finally, the Christian must not lose sight of the affirmation which expresses—in a single phrase—the uniting of God's act to man's response. Christ also suffered for you, leaving you an example, that you should follow in his steps (2:21-25). Man's response is the counterpart of God's act in Christ. The life of discipleship is patterned after God's sacrificial involvement in our world through Christ.

THE RECOVERY OF THE BIBLE

We noted in Chapter 1 that the Emperor Diocletian attempted to destroy the early Christian church by issuing an edict that all Christian Scriptures be burned. This powerful enemy of Christianity was clever enough to recognize that "the Word of God" was the unique channel through which flowed inspiration and motivation to the heart of the Christian movement. Can it be that many church members today are their church's worst enemies? Are not many succeeding in doing exactly what Diocletian knew would bring about the destruction of the church: cutting it off from its Scriptures, its roots, by their refusal to "read, learn, and inwardly digest" the word of God with diligence?

In a day when the relevance of the church is being seriously challenged, the community of faith cannot afford to have members who shut themselves off from the gospel which has created them as a church and is constantly recalling them to their mission. It is our hope that through this study some will be led toward a recovery of the Bible as the proclamation of God's saving act and accept and respond to its serious call to grown-up discipleship. It is our earnest hope that, through the renewed contact they have made with the Bible by means of this study, they will hear and respond to the call to *Christian being* and *Christian doing*.

Glossary

AMARANTH—From the Greek: unfading; an imaginary flower that never fades or dies.

APOCALYPSE—A revelation; a prophetic disclosure or announcement of the ultimate reign of God; literature written in the belief that the Second Coming of Christ was imminent, as The Revelation to John.

APOCRYPHA—Writings of doubtful authenticity or authorship. The Old Testament Apocrypha: the fourteen books of the Septuagint which are usually not found in the Protestant editions of the Bible.

ARAMAIC—A group of Semitic languages and dialects of which the most important are the Syriac, the Biblical and Palestinian Aramaic, and the Samaritan. It was the common language among Semitic peoples and was spoken by Jesus and his disciples.

BUDDHA, GAUTAMA (563?-483? B.C.) Indian Prince, philosopher, and founder of Buddhism.

Prince Siddhartha renounced the luxury of his palace (c. 533 B.C.) and became an ascetic. As Buddha, the enlightened one, he taught that supreme peace and freedom from suffering is found by discipline (renunciation of desire) and psychological and ethical self-culture.

CATECHISM—A simple book of religious instruction and belief, often in the form of questions and answers.

COSMOS—The world or the universe considered as an orderly and harmonious system; the opposite of chaos.

DIATRIBE—A literary form initiated by the Greek Cynics in their moral tracts; employing numerous imperatives and falling between a lecture and a private talk.

DIOCLETIAN—Roman emperor (A.D. 245-313) born at Dioclea in Dalmatia; at first friendly to Christians, later, probably persuaded by false accusations of their enemies, he issued an edict against Christians initiating terrible persecutions which raged for 10 years (303-313).

ENCYCLICAL—A circular letter sent to many people and places. A letter addressed by the Pope to all the Roman Catholic bishops of the world on a matter of interest to the church.

EPITOMIZE—To sum up in a brief statement; epitome, a condensed representation.

EUSEBIUS OF CAESAREA (260?-340?) — Christian Bishop of Caesarea; theologian, church historian and scholar, called "the father of ecclesiastical history"; wrote *Historia Ecclesiastica* (history of the Christian Church to 324).

GALEN—Second century Greek physician; born in Pergamos, Asia Minor. Settled in Rome A.D. 164 He wrote many treatises, of which about 100 survive. His works were regarded for many centuries as authoritative in Greek, Roman, and Arabic medical practice.

GANDHI, MAHATMA (M. K.) (1869-1948)—Indian nationalistic leader; instituted a campaign of passive resistance and civil disobedience; became president of Indian National Congress in 1925.

JUXTAPOSITION — Placement close together, side by side.

MAMMON—A word of Semitic origin meaning wealth or property; one of the fallen angels in Milton's *Paradise Lost;* a personification of riches as an evil spirit.

MANDARIN—The language of North China; the dialect used by the Chinese court and official classes under the Empire.

MISCELLANY—A medley, a collection of writings on various subjects or by various writers.

MORES—Customs; manners; fixed folkways with an ethical significance; customs or conventions which have the force of law.

ORIGEN (185-254)—Christian writer and teacher of Alexandria; a pupil of Clement; became head of a school in Caesarea; wrote a treatise on prayer, an exhortation on martyrdom, *Commentaries and Homilies,* and a defense of Christianity. He sought to work out a complete Christian philosophy based on the Scriptures.

POLESTAR—The north star; a guide; a directing or controlling principle.

RABBI—Master, lord, teacher; a preacher, a graduate of rabbinical school; a title of respect or honor conferred by the Jews on a teacher or doctor of the law.

SHEMA—Jewish affirmation in Deutronomy 6:4; Judaism's creed.

TIRADE—A long-drawn-out speech or declamatory passage, especially one marked by intemperate or censorious language.

TRAJAN (52-117)—Roman emperor and soldier, under whose reign Christians were persecuted.

TYNDALE, WILLIAM (1490?-1536) — Ordained priest; opposed by the clergy of the neighborhood where he preached in Gloucestershire, England. He resolved to translate the New Testament into English as a means of overcoming the corruption in the clergy. Finding no help in England he went to Germany where his translations of the New Testament and the Pentateuch were made directly from the Hebrew and Greek, furnishing a basis for the authorized version of the Bible. From Germany he fled to Antwerp where he was betrayed and publicly strangled and burned as a heretic in 1536.

Books for Further Reading

Helpful information on the Books of James and I Peter and the church today will be found in the following works, which may be ordered from the Cokesbury Book Store serving your territory, if in print (prices are subject to change). Your local church, public, or college libraries may be able to lend "out-of-print" books to you. *Editor.*

Scriptures

The Holy Bible: A New Translation by James Moffatt. New York: Doran, © 1926; Harper & Row, 1935.

The Holy Bible, Authorized King James Version. Philadelphia: John Winston Co., no date.

The Holy Bible, Revised Standard Version. New York: Thomas Nelson & Sons, 1952: *The New Testament* (RSV). Bantam Books, NC 169.

The Interpreter's Bible: The Holy Scriptures in the King James and Revised Standard Versions with General Articles and Introduction, Exegesis, Exposition for Each Book of the Bible, Vol. XII. (James; Peter; John; Jude; Revelation; General Articles; Indexes). Nashville: Abingdon Press, 1957.

The New English Bible: New Testament. Oxford and Cambridge: Oxford University Press and Cambridge University Press, 1961.

The New Testament in Modern English. J. B. Phillips, translator. New York: The Macmillan Co., © 1958.

The Apocrypha of the Old Testament: Revised Standard Version. New York: Thomas Nelson & Sons, 1957

James and I Peter

BARCLAY, WILLIAM. *The Letters of James and Peter.* 2nd ed. The Daily Study Bible. Philadelphia: Westminster Press, 1961. $2.50 (WP)

BEASLEY-MURRAY, GEORGE R. *General Epistles.* Bible Guides, No. 21. Nashville: Abingdon Press, 1965. $1.00 (AP)

BOWMAN, JOHN WICK. *Hebrews, James, I and II Peter.* The Layman's Bible Commentary, Vol. 24. Richmond, Va.: John Knox Press, 1962. $2.00 (JK)

GRANT, F. C., ed. "Preface to the Letter of James," and "Preface to the Letter of I Peter," *The New Testament.* Revised Standard Version. New York: Thomas Nelson & Sons for Bantam Books, Inc. New York: Bantam Books, 1962. Paper, 95 cents. Pp. 453-54.

MOFFATT, JAMES. *The General Epistles: James, Peter and Jude.* The Moffatt New Testament Commentary. New York: Harper & Bros., no date. $5.00 (HA)

REICKE, BO. *The Epistles of James, Peter, and Jude.* The Anchor Bible, Vol. 37. New York: Doubleday and Co., 1964. $5.00 (DD)

James

BLACKMAN, E. C. *The Epistle of James.* The Torch Bible Commentaries. New York: The Macmillan Co., 1957. $2.50 (MC)

CADOUX, A. T. *The Thought of St. James.* London: James Clarke and Co., Ltd., 1944. (Out of Print)

EASTON, BURTON S. and GORDON POTEAT. *The Epistle of James. The Interpreter's Bible,* Vol. XII. Nashville: Abingdon Press, © 1957. $8.75 (AP)

TASKER, R. V. G. *The General Epistle of James.* Tyndale New Testament Commentaries. Grand Rapids: Wm. B. Eerdmans Pub. Co., 1957. $2.25 (EP)

1 Peter

BEARE, F. W. *The First Epistle of Peter.* 2nd ed. Naperville, Ill.: Alec R. Allenson, Inc., 1961. (Greek text.) $5.50 (AA)

CRANFIELD, C. E. B. *The First Epistle of Peter.* Naperville Ill.: Alec R. Allenson, Inc., 1950. $3.00 (AA)

CROSS, F. L. *I Peter: A Paschal Liturgy.* London: A. R. Mowbray and Co., Ltd., 1954. (Out of Print)

HUNTER, A. M. and ELMER G. HOMRIGHAUSEN. *The First Epistle of Peter. The Interpreter's Bible,* Vol. XII. Nashville: Abingdon Press, 1957. $8.75 (AP)

REICKE, Bo. *The Disobedient Spirits and Christian Baptism: A Study of I Peter 3:19.* Copenhagen: Munksgaard, 1946. (Out of Print.)

STIBBS, ALAN M. and ANDREW F. WALLS. *The First Epistle General of Peter.* Tyndale New Testament Commentaries. Grand Rapids: Wm. B. Eerdmans Pub. Co., 1959. $3.25 (EP)

Christian Ethics

BONHOEFFER, DIETRICH. *The Cost of Discipleship.* R. H. Fuller, trans. New York: The Macmillan Co., 1960. $4.50; $1.45, paper (MC)

BOSLEY, HAROLD A. *Doing What Is Christian.* Nashville: The Graded Press, 1960. $1.00 (GI)

HALL, CAMERON P., ed. *On-the-Job Ethics: A Pioneering Analysis by Men Engaged in Six Major Occupations.* New York: Department of the Church and Economic Life, Division of Christian Life and Work, The National Council of The Churches of Christ in the U.S.A., 1963. $1.65 (NC)

KEE, HOWARD C. *Making Ethical Decisions.* Philadelphia: Westminster Press, 1957. $1.00 (WP)

KNOX, JOHN. *The Ethic of Jesus in the Teaching of the Church.* Nashville: Abingdon Press, 1961. $2.00 (AP)

MANSON, T. W. *Ethics and the Gospel.* New York: Charles Scribner's Sons, 1960. $2.75 (SC)

MOSKIN, ROBERT. "Morality U.S.A.," *Look*, Sept. 24, 1963. Reprints available from *Look*. 488 Madison Avenue, New York, N.Y., 10022. 15 cents each

PIKE, JAMES A. *Doing the Truth: A Summary of Christian Ethics.* Garden City, N. Y.: Doubleday and Co., 1955. $3.95 (DD); $1.45 paper (MC)

ROBINSON, J. A. T. *Christian Morals Today.* Philadelphia: Westminster Press, 1964. 65 cents (WP)

SHINN, ROGER L. *Tangled World.* New York: Charles Scribner's Sons, 1965. $3.00; $1.00 paper (SC)

STRINGFELLOW, WILLIAM. *Free in Obedience.* New York: Seabury Press, 1964. $2.75 (SN)

STRINGFELLOW, WILLIAM. *Private and Public Faith.* Grand Rapids: William B. Eerdmans Publishing Co., 1962. $3.00; $1.45 paper (EP)

General Reference

BUTTRICK, GEORGE A. and others, eds. *Interpreter's Dictionary of the Bible.* 4 vols. Nashville: Abingdon Press, 1962. $45.00 (AP)

GRANT, F. C., *How to Read the Bible.* New York: Collier. $.95 paper

Index of Biblical References

OLD TESTAMENT

[NOTE: *References discussed at length in James and I Peter are in boldface type.*]

Apocrypha of the Old Testament

New Testament

SERVICE CENTER
BOARD OF MISSIONS, THE METHODIST CHURCH
7820 Reading Road, Cincinnati, Ohio   45237
FE366   PRICE: $1.00   SC-009